# GROWING CALIFORNIA NATIVE PLANTS

# GROWING CALIFORNIA NATIVE PLANTS

Second Edition

REVISED AND EXPANDED

Marjorie G. Schmidt and
Katherine L. Greenberg

Drawings by Beth D. Merrick

UNIVERSITY OF CALIFORNIA PRESS
Berkeley Los Angeles London

This book is dedicated to the memory of Marjorie Schmidt (1905–1989).

---

University of California Press, one of the most distinguished university presses in the United States, enriches lives around the world by advancing scholarship in the humanities, social sciences, and natural sciences. Its activities are supported by the UC Press Foundation and by philanthropic contributions from individuals and institutions. For more information, visit www.ucpress.edu.

University of California Press
Berkeley and Los Angeles, California

University of California Press, Ltd.
London, England



Library of Congress Cataloging-in-Publication Data

Schmidt, Marjorie G.
Growing California native plants / Marjorie G. Schmidt and Katherine L. Greenberg ; drawings by Beth D. Merrick. — 2nd ed., rev. and expanded
p. cm.
First ed. published: Berkeley : University of California Press, 1980.
Includes bibliographical references and index.
ISBN 978-0-520-26668-1 (cloth : alk. paper) — ISBN 978-0-520-26669-8 (pbk. : alk. paper)
1. Native plant gardening—California. 2. Native plants for cultivation—California. 3. Plants, Ornamental—California. I. Greenberg, Katherine L. II. Merrick, Beth D. III. Title.

SB439.S33 2012
639.9'51794—dc23 2011028667

Manufactured in Singapore
19 18 17 16 15 14 13 12
10 9 8 7 6 5 4 3 2 1

The paper used in this publication meets the minimum requirements of ANSI/NISO Z39.48-1992 (R 1997) (*Permanence of Paper*).

*Front cover image:* Drought-tolerant garden and gravel patio shaded by native oaks. *Back cover image: Ceanothus,* 'Julia Phelps,' *Sidalcea malvaflora,* and *Eschscholzia californica,* Menzies Garden, Strybing Arboretum. Photos © Saxon Holt/PhotoBotanica.

The publisher gratefully acknowledges the generous support
of the General Endowment Fund of the University of
California Press Foundation.

# CONTENTS

# ACKNOWLEDGMENTS

Marjorie Schmidt made an enormous contribution to native plant horticulture in 1980 with the publication of *Growing California Native Plants*. I started growing native plants in my Lafayette garden the year Marjorie Schmidt's book was published, and it has been a valuable guide to me and to countless other gardeners for thirty years. In writing this revised edition, I have drawn from my own experiences and experiments with native plants.

Readers familiar with the original book may be surprised by the reversal of the plant chapters, from trees to annuals rather than from annuals to trees. It seemed logical to reorganize the progression of plant types in this way because trees provide an enduring framework for the garden and create environments for other plants, while annuals enliven the well-formed garden with their fleeting forms and colors. I have added a description of plant communities, native grasses, and some now-familiar plants whose horticultural potential was not recognized when the book first appeared. This edition also includes new cultivars and categories now considered more important by many gardeners, such as plants that attract wildlife.

Many people shared their knowledge of native plants and contributed to this project. My parents introduced me to the beauty of the California landscape when I was growing up in Monterey County, and this was the beginning of a lifelong fascination with native plants. The Regional Parks Botanic Garden in Berkeley has inspired me for many years, and Steve Edwards, director, generously provided many of the photographs for this book.

I wish to thank Phyllis Faber for asking me to work on this project, and the editors and production team at University of California Press for their guidance and attention to detail. Editors Kate Marshall and Kate Hoffman, editorial coordinator Lynn Meinhardt, and production editor Jean Blackburn all contributed to the quality of this book. Thanks also go to Bob Case, Nora Harlow, Saxon Holt, Nevin Smith, Phil Van Soelen, and Richard Turner. I am particularly grateful to my husband, Charles Greenberg, for his enthusiastic support of this book and the making of a native garden.

Katherine L. Greenberg

# GARDENING WITH NATIVE PLANTS

**JUAN RODRIGUEZ CABRILLO** was the first European to explore the California coast, landing on the shores of San Diego Bay in 1542. From the time the first European explorers set foot here, California became known as the land of flowers. It was named for a mythical island "very close to . . . the Terrestrial Paradise," described in a 16th-century Spanish novel by Montalvo. Spanish explorers and others who followed were amazed by this remarkable region with its diverse landscapes and flora. They soon discovered that, while some of the plants were similar to those of their homelands, many were new to them.

Three centuries later, Zenas Leonard was among the first explorers to enter California by crossing the Sierra from east to west with the Walker party. In *Narrative of the Adventures of Zenas Leonard* (1839), he noted the apparent reversal of the seasons: "as there is no winter nor freezing weather here it may be said that August, September and October, is their only winter, (to substitute *warm* for *cold*) as, at the end of this period the face of nature assumes a new dress and vegetation shoots forth precisely in the manner that it does in Pennsylvania when the frost leaves the ground in the Spring of the year."

Today this unique native flora, which gives the California landscape much of its distinctive beauty and attraction, is threatened. The rapid increase in population and land development has changed and disrupted the habitat of all wildlife, particularly of wild plants. Inflated land values and lack of planning for the future have complicated efforts to protect native species, and much has been lost from the once extensive and glorious flora of California. We can never fully replace such losses, but we can protect and encourage the use of our remaining treasure of native plants.

Mt. Diablo meadow

## The Case for Native Plants

California has a wealth of plant species, including many that are not found anywhere else, and several actions can be taken to save them. The most important is to preserve habitats by setting aside land where typical, rare, or endangered species occur in some concentration. Saving plants in their native habitats can also help them adapt to changes in temperature and rainfall patterns. On protected lands, native plants can remain undisturbed in their natural state and available for study. Living collections of representative species in horticultural institutions provide further protection for plants threatened by extinction.

Growing native plants is another way for us to connect with our natural heritage and bring the beauty of the natural landscape into our gardens. There is a native plant for any garden situation, and, properly selected, they flourish with less attention than many exotic species. Many are drought-tolerant, such as plants growing in dry foothills and other arid places. Other species come from moist habitats, including stream banks, meadows, and woodlands, and flourish in gardens with similar conditions. There are many possibilities for creating attractive and sustainable native plant gardens suited to the conditions of the site.

## Horticultural Beginnings

Learning about traditional uses deepens our appreciation of the native flora. For thousands of years, numerous tribes of Native Americans inhabited the region now called California and interacted with the native plants

Indian grinding stone with acorns

Mission San Juan Bautista

where they lived. The first European visitors to California found a park-like landscape that was the result of a long history of land management. Indigenous people practiced tilling, sowing, weeding, pruning, burning, and selective harvesting to manage plant populations and shape their natural environments. They gathered wild plants for food, medicine, basketry, clothing, and other uses. Early settlers and mission fathers learned some practical uses for native plants from the Indians, but they had little time to be concerned with wild plants. Their gardens usually contained favorite plants brought from their homelands, and they did not attempt to cultivate the unfamiliar native plants.

Interest in this flora began long before statehood, as the early explorers came to recognize the wealth of native plants. Many of California's most beautiful wild plants were brought into cultivation as early as the late 1700s, when European explorers sent seeds and cuttings to their home countries. They became highly respected garden plants, especially in England. David Douglas was one of the best known of the early botanical explorers, and he probably sent more seeds and specimens to Europe than any other person. In California, concern for native plants did not keep pace with the European enthusiasm.

The recorded history of the use of California native plants in gardens is sparse. A newcomer to the state may ask why much of the superb heritage of native plants has failed, until recently, to become popular garden material. The first nurseries, some well established by the mid-19th century, imported plants rather than encouraging the use of indigenous plants. By the early 1900s a few native trees and shrubs were considered to be worthy of a place in gardens, including coast redwood (*Sequoia sempervirens*), Matilija poppy (*Romneya coulteri*), island bush poppy (*Dendromecon harfordii*), hollyleaf cherry (*Prunus ilicifolia*), toyon (*Heteromeles arbutifolia*), evergreen sumacs (*Rhus* spp.), and several species of ceanothus.

At the same time agricultural development was advancing rapidly, attended by the introduction of exotic, and often weedy grasses, shrubs, and several trees. As a result of this, oleander, eucalyptus, and the pepper tree (*Schinus molle*) have become so firmly established that it is difficult to convince newcomers that these are not native to California. Even before this period, John Muir, the most respected of early conservationists, expressed the sentiments of many when he deplored the invasion of human activities in forests and in the "bee pastures" of the Central Valley.

Several far-sighted and dedicated people were proceeding without much fanfare to help Californians become acquainted with their wild plants. To them it seemed logical to use the plants that graced the hills and canyons, and we owe them a debt of gratitude for their persistence. These native plant enthusiasts were botanists, nurserymen, or home gardeners, most of whom did their own seed collecting and propagating. Louis Edmunds, Theodore Payne, Carl Purdy, Kate Sessions, Howard McMinn, Lester Rowntree, James Roof, Gerda Isenberg, Dara Emery, Wayne Roderick, and countless others made lasting contributions to native plant horticulture in the 20th century. Today many young horticulturists are exploring the possibilities for useful native plants, determined to fill the gaps where knowledge about them is still missing.

The early history includes several instances of rare plants being rescued from destruction. At least one was highly dramatic when the last Franciscan manzanita (*Arctostaphylos franciscana*) was snatched from the old Laurel Hill Cemetery in San Francisco by James Roof. Seventy years after this plant was thought to be extinct in the wild, a Franciscan Manzanita was found growing in the path of a freeway construction project in the Presidio and moved to a protected site. Several other rare plants have been preserved to enrich western gardens, including Nevin's barberry (*Berberis nevinii*), whose original habitat in the San Fernando Valley is now covered with houses, and Mount Vision ceanothus (*Ceanothus gloriosus* var. *porrectus*), which was nearly destroyed by the 1995 Vision Fire. A few plants that are rare and endangered in their native habitats, such as the lovely bush anemone (*Carpenteria californica*) and Vine Hill manzanita (*Arctostaphylos densiflora*), can be easily found in nurseries.

Until recently, gardeners seeking to observe native plants grown with suitable companions found few examples except in botanic gardens. Even now few nurseries carry a full complement of native plants, and the gardening public has yet to show a sustained interest in them. A lack of literature on the propagation and culture of native plants, especially from personal experience, has also worked against their becoming popular.

Santa Barbara Botanic Garden

And further, very little publicity has been given to those natives which have been refined for garden use. This is starting to change with horticultural societies, water districts, and some communities sponsoring symposia, creating demonstration gardens, and organizing garden tours to promote native plants. More nurseries are offering regionally appropriate native plants, including plants grown from locally collected seeds and cuttings. The Resources chapter offers suggestions for further reading, gardens and nurseries to visit, organizations to join, and sources of plants and seeds.

## Botanic Gardens

A major step toward a better understanding of native plants began in the 1920s with the establishment of the first botanic gardens devoted to native plants. Santa Barbara Botanic Garden was founded in 1926, followed by Rancho Santa Ana Botanic Garden in 1927. The Regional Parks Botanic Garden in Berkeley was started in 1940 with plants arranged according to geographic regions. Many universities have botanic gardens with large plant collections, which include some native ones. University of California Botanical Garden in Berkeley, established in 1891, is one of the oldest with plants from throughout the state grouped by plant communities. Leaning

Regional Parks Botanic Garden

Pine Arboretum, an outstanding demonstration garden on the California Polytechnic State University campus in San Luis Obispo, showcases plants from the world's five Mediterranean climate regions, including California. The San Francisco Botanical Garden at Strybing Arboretum in Golden Gate Park has developed an impressive California garden and an outstanding horticultural library. Most of these botanic gardens offer guided tours, education programs, and plant sales.

Much basic work in the process of selecting native plants is conducted in these institutions, although it remains on a small scale. Collecting, propagating, and growing plants takes time, and it may take many years to judge the merits of the plants being tested. Each step must be recorded to share the benefit of experience in successes or failures. Native plant research and conservation is also supported by botanic gardens. One example of this is a project to introduce Mount Diablo buckwheat (*Eriogonum truncatum*) and other rare plants on several sites to augment the existing populations from seeds collected by staff of the Regional Parks Botanic Garden and the University of California Botanical Garden. This project and similar efforts on other sites will help ensure the survival of rare and endangered plants in their native habitats.

## California Native Plant Society

Another important step toward protecting native plants was taken in 1965 with the founding of the California Native Plant Society. The mission of

CNPS is to increase understanding and appreciation of California's native plants and to conserve them and their natural habitats through education, science, advocacy, horticulture, and land stewardship. Many chapters have been organized throughout the state, and they sponsor educational programs, field trips, plant sales, and publications. Joining this society is one way to learn about native plants and become involved in preserving the wild flora.

# CALIFORNIA PLANT HABITATS

Native plants are species that existed in California before the arrival of explorers and colonists, and the great diversity of native plants results from the state's varied topography, climate, and soils. Approximately 6,300 native species, subspecies, and varieties have been identified, and new discoveries are still being made. It is notable that a third of these plants are endemic, that is, they are restricted to a single locality or habitat. Some of the rarest endemics, such as the lovely bush anemone, have been popular garden plants for years. The fame of coast redwood, the world's tallest tree, and giant sequoia, the world's largest tree, have attracted many visitors to California. The state also has a large number of native plant cultivars with outstanding qualities for gardens, and new selections are being introduced.

We cannot give more than a brief overview of the nature, distribution, and complexity of the native flora here. Certain broad features are obvious, especially the magnificent conifer forests of mountain regions and the northern coastal section of the state. Foothill regions are mostly dominated by oaks and their attendant shrubs, herbaceous plants, and grasses. Low hills, valleys, and coastal plains form vast carpets of colorful wildflowers, which bloom abundantly in spring. Drought-tolerant shrubs, forming dense thickets known as chaparral, are the dominant plants on coastal and inland mountain slopes. And some native plants are found only near watercourses and other moist places where they bloom freely over long periods to form wild gardens of great beauty.

## California Floristic Province

The California Floristic Province is a geographical region that contains the plant species that are most characteristic of the state's flora. It extends from the Oregon border to Baja California and covers most of the state from the Pacific Ocean to the crest of the Sierra Nevada as well as the area west of the Transverse and Peninsular Ranges and the Channel Islands, where many endemic species can be found. The plants described in this book are native to this unique province, which is isolated by climate and topography from the drier desert regions (Great Basin, Mojave, Colorado) of northeastern and southeastern California. The Pacific Ocean has a moderating influence on the climate, and the Sierra Nevada also influences the climate and much of the state's water supply. The Sierra Nevada separates California from the continental climate that prevails over the inland portion of the country.

Most of California west of the Sierra Nevada has a Mediterranean climate, which is characterized by warm, dry summers and cool, wet winters. Rainfall is seasonal, and periods of six months or more without rain are typical. Only five regions have this climate type, representing less than two percent of the world's land area: California, central Chile, the Mediterranean Basin, Southwestern and South Australia, and the Cape Region of South Africa. All are located on the western edge of continents between 30 and 40 degrees latitude north and south of the equator, and plants native to these summer-dry regions have similar adaptations.

Variations in temperature, rainfall, wind, and fog often occur within short distances in California, creating numerous microclimates that influence vegetation patterns. The vegetation changes as the landscape becomes drier from north to south and from the mild coastal zone to inland valleys and foothills. Fog modifies the climate along the coast during the summer months, reducing water loss from plants and soil. Away from the coast, summers are hotter and drier and winters are colder with occasional frost in inland valleys. As Lester Rowntree noted in *Hardy Californians*, "At no time of the year is *all* of California hot, or cold, or dry, or wet. The

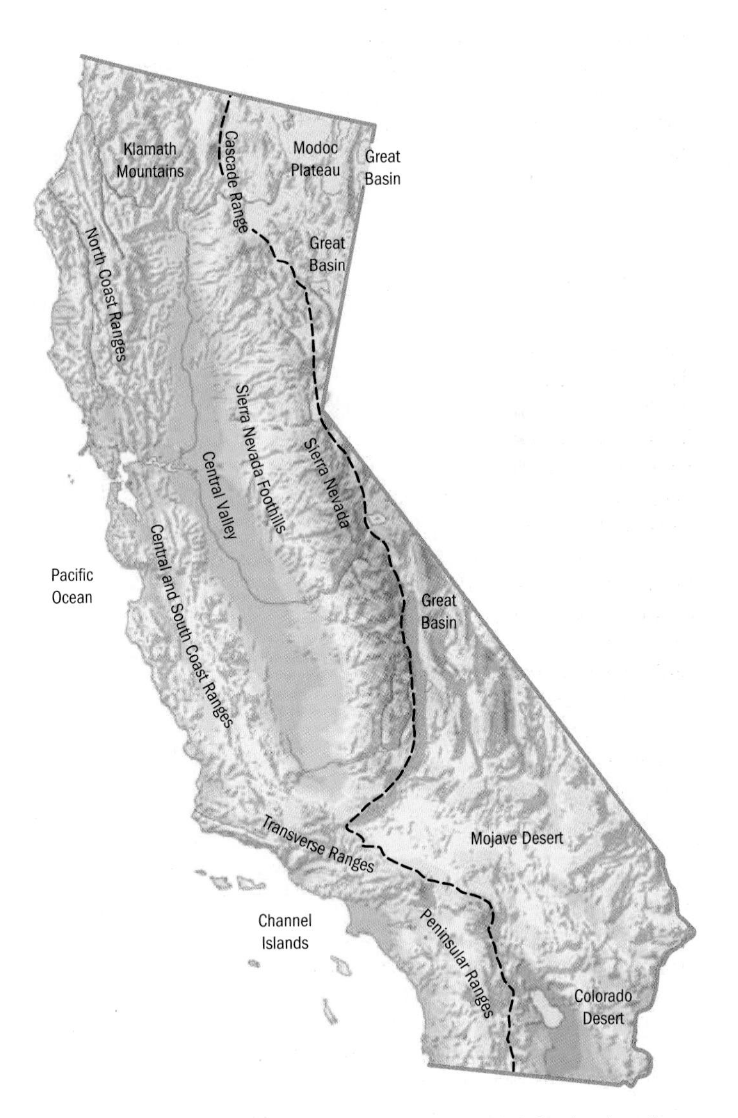


Major topographical features of California. The California Floristic Province is on the coastward side of the hatched line.

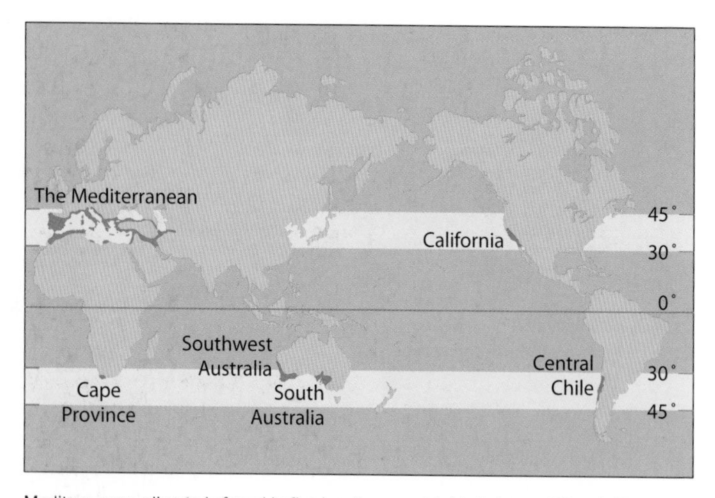


Mediterranean climate is found in five locations worldwide between 30 and 45 degrees latitude as shown in red. Scale reflects distances at equator.

southern end—that part best known to visitors—may be parching in drought and heat while the north is drenched in rain."

The state's winter rainfall comes from storm systems that develop over the Pacific Ocean and move inland, and rainfall decreases from northern to southern California. Annual rainfall averages over fifty inches on the western slopes of the Coast Ranges and the Sierra Nevada to as little as ten inches in the San Joaquin Valley and southern California. It can exceed one hundred inches in Del Norte County, and the drier desert regions that extend beyond the eastern border of the state (Great Basin, Colorado, Mojave) receive less ten inches of rain per year. Precipitation in the higher mountains throughout the state takes the form of snow.

The absence and abundance of water are recurring themes in the history of California. John Steinbeck famously recalled in *East of Eden*, "And it never failed that during the dry years the people forgot about the rich years, and during the wet years they lost all memory of the dry years. It was always that way." Growing up in "Steinbeck Country" I heard many conversations about the rain, or lack of it, and stories about my great-grandparents who were dry farmers (growing crops without irrigation) in the early years of the 20th century. We went hiking in the hills and valleys of Monterey County and enjoyed spectacular displays of wildflowers in years of abundant rainfall. These experiences, together with extended drought cycles in recent years, have given me a greater appreciation for the importance of water in California.

Dry years are normal in California, and one of the most severe droughts of the 20th century occurred from 1929 to 1934. The importance of practicing water conservation in gardening was recognized during another severe drought in the 1970s, and more attention was given to native plants. Observation of plants in the wild during this dry period showed that many species accepted unaccustomed drought without permanent damage, although in some cases there was wilting, early drop of foliage, or an early dormant period. For the last few decades, utility companies and botanic gardens throughout the state have been promoting drought-tolerant native plants and climate-compatible gardening through publications, classes, and demonstration gardens.

Plants adapted to a Mediterranean climate have various strategies for surviving summer drought. Annuals complete their life cycle by setting seed before summer begins, and many bulbs and grasses go dormant during the dry season. Most chaparral plants are also summer-dormant, and this reduces their need for water during the dry months. A number of drought-tolerant species have thick leaves with waxy coatings to reduce moisture loss, and some plants have two sets of roots for capturing moisture—a deep tap root and lateral roots closer to the surface. Many manzanitas hold their leaves in a distinctive, vertical position to reduce exposure to sunlight, and buckeyes are drought-deciduous, losing their leaves in summer.

Fire is a natural event in California, and it contributes to a greater diversity of vegetation types. Many plants have evolved with periodic fires, and some require fire to complete their life cycles. Chaparral shrubs have adaptations that enable them to survive and regenerate after fire. Some wildflowers only appear after a fire, and the seed cones of Monterey pines and other closed-cone pines only open after fire. Native Americans used fire to manage their environment and increase populations of food plants and wildlife. In the 20th century, fire suppression policies reduced the frequency of fires, which led to more intense and damaging fires, especially in the canyons and foothills of central and southern California. Yet an impressive number of native shrubs and trees, including bays and oaks, in the Santa Barbara Botanic Garden were showing new growth soon after a devastating fire swept through Mission Canyon in 2009.

California's varied topography is another factor that influences the distribution of native vegetation. Coastal scrub and chaparral typically grow on hot, dry, south- or west-facing slopes, and cooler, shaded north-facing slopes with deeper soils support forests and woodlands. Redwood forests are characteristic of the northwestern coastal section of the state, while in other places conifers are mixed with broadleaved trees. Grasslands are found in coastal plains, valleys, and rolling hills. Many of the native plants in cultivation derive from California's coastal areas and from the state's most extensive geographical feature, the foothills. Adaptable plants also come from moist meadows and stream banks. Plants from these areas, along with a few from localized places, are the easiest natives to grow in most California gardens. Plants restricted to rock crevices and ledges, serpentine slopes, and bogs often require special attention when brought into cultivation.

## Plant Communities

Botanists have long studied natural associations of plants, and various classification systems have been worked out over the years. A plant community is an assemblage of plant species, which grow together where conditions of climate, slope, and soil are similar. For more information, readers can refer to *The Jepson Manual* or *Introduction to California Plant Life*, by Robert Ornduff.

California's major plant communities or vegetation types include chaparral, coastal scrub, grassland, woodland, riparian woodland, and forest. Species composition varies from place to place, and some species occur in more than one plant community. The natural landscape is a complex mosaic of vegetation where chaparral can be found growing near grasslands, oak woodlands, and redwood forests.

Plant communities can serve a useful guide to plant selection because plants that grow together in the wild make good companions in the garden. Gardens with variations in slope, exposure, and soils can showcase plants from several plant communities. Chaparral shrubs and drifts of native grasses and sages thrive in the open, sunny areas of my garden, and a grove of vine maples suited to the shady, north side of the house features an understory of ferns and western bleeding heart. The north-facing hillside above and below the house is planted with oaks and plants adapted to dry shade, and the creek area at the base of the slope is a natural riparian woodland that provides habitat for wildlife and a cool retreat in summer.

### Chaparral

One of California's most characteristic plant communities, chaparral forms a dense cover of tough, mainly evergreen shrubs on hot, dry, south- or west-facing, and often inaccessible, slopes with shallow soils. The name *chaparral* is Spanish for "place of scrub oak." In *Flowering Shrubs of California*, Lester Rowntree described chaparral as "a thick evergreen blanket, very soft to the distant eye, very resistant at close range, covering miles upon miles of southern California's hills." Manzanita, ceanothus, silktassel bush, toyon, coffeeberry, and sugar bush are garden-worthy chaparral shrubs. They provide a strong foundation for dry gardens, and their flowers and fruits add seasonal interest.

Chaparral vegetation

Coastal scrub vegetation

## Coastal Scrub

Also called "soft chaparral," coastal scrub is noted for its low, soft-leaved shrubs and perennials, including many with aromatic foliage. Plants of this community are drought-tolerant and prefer full sun, but occasional watering in the late summer and early fall will improve their appearance in gardens. Coastal scrub has different associations in northern and southern California. Dominated by evergreen species, northern coastal scrub occurs along coastal bluffs from Big Sur to Oregon. This area is home to a

Valley grassland with vernal pool

number of plants suitable for coastal and inland gardens, such as coyote brush, bush monkeyflower, blue blossom, coast buckwheat, California sunflower, coffeeberry, and some manzanitas. Farther south, buckwheats, sages, sagebrush, and golden yarrow are common, with coastal sage scrub growing on bluffs and rocky slopes from Big Sur into Baja California. This plant community consists of a number of drought-deciduous perennials, including many with silver-gray foliage, that combine well with native grasses and chaparral shrubs.

## Grassland

Grassland once covered large areas of California's hills and valleys. Although many of the native species have been replaced by nonnative annual grasses and reduced by land development and agriculture, native grasses can still be found in many places throughout the state. When rainfall is abundant, there are dazzling displays of wildflowers in California's grasslands. Vernal pools are shallow seasonal wetlands found in valley grasslands and characterized by colorful rings of spring wildflowers, such as meadowfoam and gold fields, that appear in succession as the water evaporates. A mixture of grasses, annual wildflowers, and bulbs makes an eye-catching meadow garden.

## Woodland

Foothills and canyons are favored by open woodlands, dominated by the rounded canopies of oaks growing with buckeyes and gray pines. Native

Oak woodland

oaks are protected trees in many residential areas, with older trees reaching impressive proportions. A number of landscape oaks have grown from acorns planted by squirrels and scrub jays, and oak seedlings frequently appear in gardens where there is an oak tree nearby. Adapted to California's summer-dry climate, plants that tolerate dry shade, such as evergreen currant, hummingbird sage, snowberry, and coffeeberry, are the natural companions of oaks. Grassland and chaparral often occur near oak woodland.

## Riparian Woodland

Flying over California, green ribbons of riparian vegetation, composed mainly of deciduous trees growing along rivers and streams, can be seen winding their way through canyons and valleys. Alders, maples, cottonwoods, willows, black walnuts, and California sycamores are found in these riparian corridors with wild grape, clematis, and honeysuckle. California wild rose, snowberry, wood fern, ninebark, sedges, and rushes also grow along shaded stream banks and in gardens with similar conditions. Riparian plants are adapted to moist conditions, although some of these plants, such as snowberry and wood fern, will also tolerate dry shade.

## Forest

Redwood forest thrives in northern California's fog belt from Monterey County to the Oregon border. Farther inland beyond the reach of summer fog, forests dominated by coast redwoods transition to mixed evergreen

Riparian woodland

Redwood forest

forest. Here Douglas firs, madrones, bays, and live oaks grow with black oaks and bigleaf maples in various combinations. Redwood sorrel, wild ginger, inside-out flower, western sword fern, salal, huckleberry, Pacific wax myrtle, and vine maple are outstanding landscape plants associated with northern California's forests, and all prefer shade and some moisture in gardens. Closed-cone pine forest occurs sporadically along the coast from Santa Barbara County northward and includes beach pine, Monterey pine, and Monterey cypress.

# DESIGNING A NATIVE GARDEN

Native plants can have a place in every kind of garden and landscape situation. This chapter is intended to aid gardeners by suggesting procedures and examples gleaned from personal observation and experience. Perhaps this chapter should be called "making the most of the environment" because it makes a strong appeal to preserve existing native plants where possible, and to create a pleasing garden suited to the climate and conditions of the site.

## Getting Started

Designing a native garden begins with an assessment of the site—its microclimates, the amount and timing of light and shade, availability of moisture, soils, slopes, and wind patterns. It is important to decide how a garden will be used before laying out areas for planting, spaces for outdoor living, and habitats for wildlife. The architecture of the house, views, drainage, and grading also influence the design of a garden. A scaled drawing of the garden showing the location of buildings, hard landscape features, and existing plants is the basis for developing a planting plan. Putting the plan on paper makes it easier to be selective and to determine the numbers and sizes of plants needed to complete the design. Final adjustments to the placement of plants can be made at the time of planting.

If you are fortunate enough to find remnants of wild flora or a natural rock outcrop on your property, it is practical and logical to incorporate them into the garden. Some invasive plants or brush may have to be removed, but a careful survey of existing plants should be made before removing any plants. One of the common tragedies in California is the devastating removal of all plants, which results in dry, exposed soil open to weed invasion and erosion. It can take years to restore soils cleared of plant material and heavily graded during construction of homes and subdivisions.

Where native vegetation remains, it should be observed over a period of several seasons to discover useful or ornamental plants. A new season may bring colonies of annuals or bulbs. Where trees and shrubs occur, they should be retained, if possible, to create a framework for the garden. Pruning may be necessary to improve the appearance of existing plants, and this should be done over time to achieve the best results. Tree seedlings and large shrubs may have awkward or dead limbs or be straggly in appearance, but they will emerge as useful plants when trimmed or thinned. It may be desirable to clear away dead or overhanging branches or to open views of a "borrowed" landscape beyond the garden.

For the newcomer to California, or the beginner who knows little of native plants, the ideal way to get acquainted with native plants is to observe them in the wild or in gardens. A visit to a native nursery might suggest possibilities or reveal a new plant introduction. You will gain practical information by keeping a record of your observations, such as when different species begin to bloom and what plant combinations are appealing. Always spend time observing a plant and its habits before bringing it into your garden. Gathering information about the mature size and horticultural requirements of each plant will help you make informed decisions about plant selection.

## Plant Selection and Design

Native plants can be used in small, enclosed urban gardens or in large, rural or semi-rural gardens that blend with the natural landscape. Plants with refined habits are suitable for formal gardens, and there are many possible choices for naturalistic gardens. Even in relatively small gardens, formal elements, such as vine-covered pergolas and symmetrical plantings, can be combined with informal features that might include a wildflower meadow or a seasonal creek.

A well-designed garden is more than a collection of plants, although a collection of sages or ceanothus could be the starting point for a native garden. Plants repeated throughout a garden or along a path create a sense of rhythm and unity, while a well-placed specimen can become a focal point or accent. The colors and textures of flowers, foliage, and bark add seasonal interest. Flowers are often fleeting, but the forms and foliage of trees and shrubs can sustain a garden throughout the year. The rounded forms of manzanitas and oaks evoke the contours of California's hills and valleys, and grasses are outstanding for textural contrasts. Plants with aromatic foliage, such as sages and Catalina perfume, and edible natives like strawberries and miner's lettuce, add to the enjoyment of a native garden.

Ornamental plants should have some, or maybe all, of the following qualifications: attractive form, foliage of good substance and color, flowers in appealing colors or in abundance to enhance the plant, decorative fruits or seed vessels, and interest in one or more seasons of the year. These features should be combined with a neat appearance, nonrampant growing habits, and wildlife value. Plants should also be adaptable to cultivation or accepting of garden conditions and compatible in terms of cultural requirements. For some species, special requirements may have to be satisfied, such as selected exposure, special soils, or the need for a dormant period.

Creating compatible combinations is one of the keys to successful cultivation of native plants, and knowing a plant's natural habitats and tolerances can help with selection. Deciduous and evergreen species may be combined by choosing plants whose bare branches or leaf emergence will complement each other. Plants with silver-gray leaves make striking accents and add a delightful contrast to plants with dark green foliage. Pleasing combinations of colors and textures, whether subtle or showy, are practically endless. Suggestions for suitable companion plants are made throughout this book, and gardeners are encouraged to experiment with other possibilities.

The size of the garden influences the scale and number of plants, and placement of plants is determined by their ultimate size and growth rate. Plants of a permanent character, such as trees and shrubs, are generally chosen first to define the structure of a garden, but a selection of grasses might be the primary consideration when designing a native meadow. Perennials, annuals, and bulbs can be added, choosing appropriate species to complete the design. Some plants will need to be removed or replaced as conditions change, and short-lived plants are useful for filling spaces between shrubs and trees that may take years to mature.

Native garden inspired by the natural landscape

Gardens change over time, sometimes in unexpected ways, providing many opportunities for refinements. Taking photos or keeping a journal can be useful for evaluating the progress of a garden throughout the year and creating future plans. We can learn from our successes as well as from our failures, and a plant that is not suited to one location may do well in another. Microclimates within a garden make it possible to grow a variety of plants adapted to different conditions or to try a plant in more than one garden situation. Fall is the ideal time to augment existing plantings, replace plants that are not thriving, or install a new garden.

## Seasonal Effects

The flowering season in California begins with the rains, and a well-planned garden can include a succession of blooms throughout the year. Manzanitas start blooming as early as October or November, and elegant, silver catkins decorate coast silk-tassel branches in January for a delightful winter effect. Redbud is spectacular in early spring when its bare branches seem to burst into bloom with clusters of brilliant pink flowers. The fame of wild lilacs is legendary, and California's exquisite wildflowers, too numerous to mention here, light up the garden in spring. And just when the last of the spring-blooming wildflowers are fading, California fuchsias come into their own in mid-summer to brighten the garden until late fall.

There is a change in the quality of light toward the end of summer as the days become shorter and cooler, and this is the time of year when the subtle colors and textures of foliage and bark can be most appreciated. A variety of seeds and berries also add interest to autumn garden. The feathery seeds of mountain mahogany glow in the afternoon sun, tawny grasses weave through the garden, catching the light and each passing breeze, and golden pear-shaped fruits hang from the branch tips of buckeyes. The pale, bare branches of buckeyes are stunning against a background of evergreen oaks in autumn and winter, and toyons enliven the winter landscape with their bright red berries.

These and other plants with ornamental fruits, cones, and seeds are listed in the Plant Selection Guide. Some plants are outstanding in every season, and I would put manzanitas at this top of this list. They merit attention for their foliage and bark alone, not to mention their delicate flowers and edible fruits. In *Native Treasures,* Nevin Smith wrote, "Few native plant groups are as symbolic of the California landscape as the manzanitas. Even for the casual traveler, they conjure images of the chaparral at its flowering best in early spring, and of its soft colors and textures at other times."

## Nature as Inspiration

Interest in the natural environment has led to a wider use of native plants. A garden inspired by nature is generally informal, but not unrestrained. Such a garden should follow a plan, using design principles, such as line, scale, balance, and unity. Simplicity is the hallmark of some of the most successful designs, and it can also be the greatest challenge for the exuberant gardener when there are so many possibilities to consider. It is easier to create a garden around remnants of native flora, but a native garden can be designed on any site with a thoughtful selection of plants. The starting point could be a shady area under an old oak with an assemblage of woodland plants or a rock outcrop on which a collection of buckwheats or sages will find sun and well-drained soil to their liking.

I started my Lafayette garden thirty years ago on a bare, north-facing hillside, which had been cleared of nonnative annual grasses. A year-round creek meanders through the property at the base of the slope. Plants were selected to enhance the existing riparian vegetation and to reflect the character of the oak woodlands, chaparral, and grasslands in the surrounding hills. A shady area on the north side of the house provided an ideal microclimate for a grove of vine maples with an understory of plants from the redwood forest plant community. The character of the garden has changed and evolved as young trees and shrubs have matured, and some of the original plants have been replaced with others that are better suited to changing conditions of sun and shade.

A smaller garden could feature plants from a single plant community or vegetation type. A windswept garden near the sea would be an ideal

Weathered bench in a native garden

place for plants from coastal sage scrub or coastal prairie, while a hillside garden in an inland valley might be the perfect setting for plants adapted to chaparral or oak woodlands. Local field stones or lichen-covered boulders could be added for accents, walls, and edges for plants and paths. A weathered bench along a stepping stone path or under a spreading oak makes an inviting place to linger in a native garden. One of the benches in my garden is shaded by a large bay tree near the creek, and it is especially pleasant on warm summer days. A sunny, sheltered sitting area under the bare branches of a vine maple could be equally inviting on a cool winter day.

Marjorie Schmidt created a semi-dry border on her mountain property at 3,000 feet elevation in the northwest Coast Ranges to test the drought tolerance of desirable local natives and others with the same qualifications from elsewhere. This section of her garden had a southwestern tilt and sun for most of the day. Volunteer oaks were growing here and there with coyote mint, irises, manzanitas, and madrones. Lupines and penstemons were added for their handsome foliage and flowers in vibrant shades of blue and purple. A few rooted cuttings of Sonoma sage were set out to meander through the foreground plantings together with a treasury of native bulbs that thrived with sun, lean soil, and a dormant period in late summer. This garden was nearly self-sufficient and required little attention other than a

Leaf litter as mulch

deep watering every two weeks from the end of the rainy season until mid-July, allowing for seed setting, and the removal of dead flowers and foliage.

In practically every region of California, gardens can be made with local natives enhanced by further selections to suit the situation and garden design. Suggested plantings for a number of garden situations are included in the Plant Selection Guide.

## Sustainable Gardens

Sustainable gardens demonstrate a commitment to preserving the environment for present and future generations. Much can be learned from the land management practices used by Native Americans as we strive to create enduring gardens that connect us to this unique place called California. In *Tending the Wild,* M. Kat Anderson notes that "indigenous people in California developed ways of using natural resources to meet human needs without degrading the ecological basis for their renewal. Indeed, California Indians found it possible to be both users and benefactors of native plant and animal populations."

It makes sense to create gardens that promote conservation of native plants, water, and other natural resources, while protecting wildlife and reducing waste. Designing a sustainable garden begins with an analysis of the garden site, taking note of its features and qualities. Understanding the climate, soils, and topography of the site and observing how sunlight, wind, and water move through the garden will inform decisions about planting. Making the most of available resources includes using local and recycled materials in creative ways rather than discarding them. Permeable paving and purposeful grading are useful for conserving water and directing it to where it is most needed. Fallen leaves add attractive patterns and textures, and they can be used as mulch to conserve moisture. A vine-covered pergola or the canopy of a spreading oak can provide welcome shade in summer as well as food and shelter for wildlife throughout the year.

A sustainable garden works in harmony with the natural systems of the site and helps regenerate the living systems of which we are a part. It meets the needs of the present without affecting the ability of future generations to meet their needs. With thoughtful planning, a sustainable and enduring garden can be visually pleasing, manageable, and responsible.

## Waterwise Gardens

Interest in dry gardens has increased with recurring drought cycles in California and with a growing population and agriculture competing for limited water supplies. Many native plants adapted to California's summer-dry climate can survive extended periods of drought, making them ideal candidates for waterwise gardens. Some of our most popular garden plants come from other regions of the world with a summer-dry climate, and many are compatible with California natives. A mix of native and nonnative plants can be appealing in a dry garden.

Steps can be taken to transition to a beautiful and sustainable waterwise landscape by devoting sections of a garden to drought-tolerant natives or replacing a water-consuming lawn with plants that require little or no summer irrigation once established. Fall planting saves water by taking advantage of winter rains, and a layer of mulch helps retain moisture. Many native plants, even the most drought-tolerant, may need some irrigation for the first few summers, and supplemental water should be given in winter if rains are scant. Plants that require year-round water can be used in naturally moist places like seeps and stream banks.

## Gardens for Wildlife

Gardens with a variety of native plants attract an abundance of wildlife. Hours of enjoyment will follow, whether you plant a few appropriate spe-

Bird bath with *Iris douglasiana* 'Canyon Snow'

cies or devote an entire garden to attracting wildlife. Flowers, tiers of foliage, cavities in trees, crevices under bark, and fallen logs provide nectar, forage, cover, and nesting sites for different species of birds, butterflies, and other creatures. With care and attention, gardeners can provide backyard habitats for wildlife.

Some of California's most beautiful and colorful wildflowers coevolved with hummingbirds, butterflies, and native bees. A garden of manzanitas, sages, and California fuchsias will provide a year-round source of nectar for resident hummingbirds, and plants with edible fruits and seeds will attract a variety of birds and mammals. Butterflies favor sunny, sheltered areas and native plants for nectar and food. Adults searching for nectar are attracted to flowers that are flat-topped or clustered with short flower tubes, and they lay their eggs on the host plants that serve as larval food for caterpillars. Leaf litter and mulch benefit mycorrhizal fungi, insects, frogs, and lizards, and some bare soil should be preserved for ground-nesting native bees.

Water is essential for all wildlife, and it can take the form of a small basin, creek, or pond. Harmful chemicals should be avoided to maintain a healthy environment for butterflies, birds, and mammals. Using a selection of deer-resistant plants makes it possible to create a garden without fences, as I have done in Lafayette. Deer wander through my garden, following well-worn paths to the creek. I enjoy watching these graceful animals at close range, and on one occasion I was approached by a very young fawn while its mother stood nearby. Unexpected and magical moments like these are a never-ending source of delight.

## Meadows

A well-designed meadow can be an attractive and satisfying alternative to a traditional lawn. Surrounding a meadow with trees and shrubs creates a sense of enclosure as well as contrasting areas of sun and shade. Using a selection of perennial grasses from coastal prairies or foothill grasslands is ideal for creating meadows suited to coastal or inland environments. Red fescue, tufted hairgrass, Cape Mendocino reedgrass, and California meadow sedge are found in coastal prairies, while needlegrass, California fescue, and deer grass occur in warmer and drier foothill grasslands. Stunning effects can be achieved by planting native grasses alone or by combining them with annual and perennial wildflowers. Managing a native meadow requires diligent weeding, occasional irrigation, and periodic cutting or mowing.

## Fire-Safe Landscaping

Many people enjoy living along the urban-wildland boundary in California with its ecosystem of grasslands, chaparral, and woodlands—vegetation types that are adapted to periodic fires. Fire-suppression policies have increased the risk of wildfires because they prevent the lower density fires that used to occur naturally every ten to thirty years in California. The potential for devastating fires has also increased as a result of population growth and development in fire-prone areas. In drought years, there is a long fire season with greater risk to people and property.

Living in a fire-prone area requires a thoughtful approach to landscape design, plant selection, construction materials, and maintenance. Firebreaks help prevent the spread of fires, and occasional irrigation keeps plants hydrated to resist burning. Defensible space standards recommend a thirty-foot zone of low-growing vegetation around a residence, and a larger reduced fuel zone that is determined by the location, slope, and vegetation type. Dry brush should be cleared, and trees and shrubs should be pruned to remove dead branches and layers of vegetation that have the potential to become fire ladders. Plants that are highly flammable should be kept away from homes and other structures. Consult your local fire district for guidance with vegetation management and planting recommendations.

# PROPAGATION AND PLANTING

Finding a source of native plants and seeds often begins with a visit to nurseries and botanic gardens that specialize in native plants. Some specialty nurseries stock unusual native plants or are in touch with collectors of wild plant seeds. Other sources are the plant societies devoted to a single genus, such as wild forms of lilies or irises. Many nurseries stock cultivars, which are apt to give a good garden performance, along with some of the adaptable species.

A cultivar, or cultivated variety, is a named selection made from variations among wild species or by hybridizing for superior form, flower or leaf color, garden tolerance, disease resistance, or vigor. Cultivars are usually maintained by cuttings or other vegetative methods, such as layering or division, to retain their characteristics because growing from seed often produces variation among the offspring. Some of the best cultivars have been admired and widely planted for many years, including 'Howard

McMinn' manzania and 'Julia Phelps' ceanothus, while others fall out of favor or are replaced by new and improved selections.

Botanic gardens and native plant societies can be a source of rare and unusual plants and seeds. Plants that are grown in small quantities may not be available in a given year, but some nurseries will take advance orders for large projects and contract-grown plants. Some suppliers, such as Native Here Nursery in Berkeley, specialize in collecting and propagating site-specific plants for gardens and restoration projects. A list of nurseries and seed suppliers is included the Resources chapter of this book.

Purchasing native plants and seeds from reputable sources will help ensure the survival of plants in the wild. It is illegal in California to collect plants, cuttings, or seeds on most public lands without a permit, and collecting on private property requires permission from the owner. Digging can deprive both would-be growers and nature of the seed that would have been produced, and plants transplanted from the wild often have a poor survival rate.

Propagation may be the best way to obtain native plants that are grown in small quantities by nurseries. Professional growers use greenhouses, propagating beds with bottom heat, and misting devices to insure good seed germination and rooting of cuttings. The suggestions given here for propagating native plants are geared to the home gardener. Manuals or local propagators can be consulted for further details and recommended treatments, and the International Plant Propagators Society (IPPS) has a website with useful information: www.ipps.org.

## Propagation by Seed

Growing plants from seed offers several advantages. Plants can be produced in quantity, and there is always the possibility of obtaining superior forms. Each seed holds the potential for a new flower color, leaf type, texture, or color; and even for a new plant size or shape. In the wild, seeds typically mature in late summer or fall, germinate with the winter rain, and grow in spring. Following these natural cycles in the garden usually produces the best results.

Learning to recognize garden-worthy natives by their seed vessels and collecting seed at the best time can be an adventure and not just a practical necessity. Collected seed should be dried and cleaned, placed in envelopes or bags, labeled, and dated. If seeds must be held for more than one season, they should be stored in the refrigerator. Seeds of most species can be stored for two or three years.

Growing any plant from seed begins with its germination, and the gardener will soon discover that the time required varies among the species. Oaks, buckeyes, and maples have short-lived seeds that must be sown within a few weeks of harvesting, while some lupines have seeds that remain viable for decades. All seeds require adequate moisture to sprout, and the best results usually come from sowing seeds in autumn at the beginning of the rainy season.

A large proportion of native plants germinate readily without pretreatment of seed, including most annuals and bulbs, a number of perennials, and some trees and shrubs. Some require special treatment—scarification, hot water, mulch, stratification, acid—to break the seed coat and begin germination. Annuals and bulbs usually require a cool period to germinate. Observation of how seeds germinate in the wild will give clues on procedure. Alternate freezing and thawing, wetting and drying, buffeting of seeds by the wind and rain, and fire are some of the ways seed coats are penetrated. To these can be added cold stratification, hot water, and chemicals.

Seeds can be broadcast into open ground, but many plants get a better start when they are sown in containers and later transplanted into the garden. Special soil mixes are seldom required for germinating seeds of native plants. A packaged potting soil or a mixture of equal parts of peat moss and perlite or vermiculite can be used as a germination medium. Clean containers and tools with a solution of one part bleach to five parts water before using them to prevent contamination.

The potting soil should be moist and evenly distributed to about one inch below the rim of the container or flat. Scatter the seeds thinly or sow in rows, and cover them with the soil mixture so that the seeds are no longer visible. A light covering of sphagnum moss is often recommended for very fine seeds. Keep the seeds moist until they germinate in a sheltered place away from direct sunlight.

As soon as green leaves show, move the container to a place with morning sun. When seedlings have a second or third pair of leaves, they are ready to be thinned and transplanted into gallon cans or deep, narrow tubes. Water thoroughly after transplanting, and keep seedlings shaded for a few days until the danger of wilt has passed. The transplants will be ready for planting when their roots are developed and before they become matted or coiled in the container. Although fertilizer is seldom necessary for natives, a slow-release fertilizer may be used for young plants.

## Propagation by Vegetative Methods

Plants produced by vegetative propagation methods (cuttings, divisions, offsets, layering) reach maturity faster than plants grown from seed, and this is the only way to increase stocks of plants that might not reproduce their desirable characteristics from seed. Many gardeners prefer to grow selected plants or cultivars of reliable color, habit, and culture. Vegetative propagation creates genetically identical plants that retain the traits of their parent plant.

## Propagation by Cuttings

Many kinds of woody, semiwoody, and herbaceous plants can be induced to root from cuttings under the right conditions. These include taking cuttings at the correct time and using hormones, a sterile rooting medium, and misting as well as bottom heat for some that are difficult to root. Cuttings of most plants are taken in summer or fall from vigorous, healthy tips without flower buds. Fall or winter is the best time to take cuttings from many manzanitas and ceanothus.

Take tip pieces of about three inches with a node at the base, and remove leaves from the lower portion. A mixture of equal parts of peat moss and clean, sharp sand or perlite can be used as a rooting medium. Place the medium in shallow pots or flats to suit the number of cuttings and moisten it. Dip cuttings in a rooting hormone, insert them in the medium, and water with a fine spray. A good method for the gardener who has only a few cuttings is to use a four- to six-inch pot enclosed in a plastic bag to maintain humidity, opening it daily for ventilation.

Keep the cuttings in a warm, shaded place until they have rooted and new leaves appear. The medium should be moist but not saturated. If a cutting shows signs of disease, it should be removed to prevent it from infecting others. As soon as sturdy roots have formed, transplant cuttings into containers filled with a standard soil mix. Water thoroughly and gradually expose young plants to more light. They are ready for planting out when roots are well-developed. The complete process of rooting, transplanting, and final planting may take up to a year or longer for woody plants.

Rooting of semiwoody or herbaceous materials is usually faster and more successful than for woody plants, and the procedures are the same. Several popular garden perennials are easy to propagate by cuttings, including species of *Penstemon, Monardella, Salvia,* and *Mimulus.* Cuttings taken from the thick, woody caudex of *Heuchera* species will root and provide new plants within a year's time.

## Propagation by Divisions or Offsets

Many native grasses and species that spread by rhizomes are easily divided. Division is also useful for propagating bulbs and corms. Plants that form rooted offsets or natural divisions, such as iris and strawberry, can be separated and replanted at the optimum time, generally in late fall. Snowberry and other thicket-forming shrubs have rooted sections that can be transplanted. Water plants well before dividing them, and continue watering the divisions until they are established. Most divisions can be planted directly into the ground.

## Propagation by Layering

Layering is a method of increasing plants by pegging a plant firmly to the ground until roots form. Rooted pieces are then detached from the parent plant and replanted where wanted. Layering is used for plants that produce branches at or near the ground level and are known to root in this manner.

One of the joys of gardening is to discover a layered plant, which often occurs naturally in moist, semi-shaded areas, especially where there is a buildup of leaf mold. Catalina perfume, California grape, and trailing manzanitas frequently produce new plants in this manner.

## Planting

Natives can be planted at any time of year, but late fall is the best time to plant when the days are cooler and the rainy season is beginning. This gives plants time to develop a healthy root system over the winter that will sustain them through the dry season with less irrigation. Trees and shrubs planted from one- to five-gallon containers generally overtake plants grown from larger containers after a few years and often have a higher survival rate. Many perennials are fast-growing, and they often bloom the first season when planted from four-inch pots or one-gallon cans.

Planting techniques are the same for most natives. The planting hole should be the same depth as the container and twice the width. Making the sides of the hole uneven rather than smooth allows for better root penetration into the native soil. For soils that require amendment, a mix of one-third compost and two-thirds native soil can be used. Fill the planting hole with water and allow it to drain two or three times before planting.

Water the plant before removing it from the container, and gently separate or score matted roots so they will grow into the soil. Set the root ball into the hole so the root crown is one inch higher than the finished grade. A wire basket can be used if protection from gophers is needed. Replace the soil around the plant, gently tamp it down, and water thoroughly. A top dressing of mulch around the exposed root crown will help conserve moisture. If a basin or raised berm is used for summer watering, it should be broken down as soon as autumn rains begin.

Most natives get the all nutrients they need from the soil, and fertilizer can stimulate some plants to grow too quickly and shorten their life span. If the soil is infertile due to grading or other factors, a slow-release fertilizer can be applied at the time of planting. Plants grown in containers require a container with drainage holes, an organic potting soil, and fertilizer to replace nutrients that are leached from the soil by frequent watering. Mulching helps conserve moisture, and succulents in containers benefit from a top dressing of gravel.

# TENDING A NATIVE GARDEN

The native plants of California are tremendously diverse because they evolved in a wide variety of microclimates and soils. Many of these plants, even those native to dry hills and chaparral, are tolerant of garden conditions. When trying to grow any plant, it is important to consider many aspects of its culture. These include water and drainage, drought tolerance, soil, mulch, weed control, pest and disease control, pruning, and adaptability. Time spent tending a native garden provides an opportunity to study the garden, develop ideas for new plantings, and observe seasonal changes.

Tending a native garden can often be approached on a seasonal basis rather than on a strict weekly or monthly schedule, particularly if the design of the garden is informal (without plants that require regular clipping and mowing) and plants are established. The major requirements of a successful maintenance program include fall planting to take advantage of winter rains, supplemental irrigation as needed during the dry season, mulching to suppress weeds and removal of weeds when they first appear, and pruning after flowering or during the dormant period. Working in a native garden and observing it throughout the year, with special attention to young plants and seedlings, can add to one's enjoyment of it.

## Sustainable Gardening Practices

Native plants suited to the climate and conditions of a site will thrive with less irrigation, fertilizer, and care than many non-native garden plants require. Fall planting further reduces the need for watering young plants once the winter rains begin and helps them establish a deep root system to survive the stress of summer drought. Keeping leaf litter in place or adding a layer of mulch helps retain moisture and cool the soil, while suppressing weeds and returning organic material to the soil. Composting also converts organic waste, such as leaves and clippings, into a nutrient-rich soil amendment. My approach has been to let leaves and twigs decompose in place as they do in nature rather than placing them in a bin or other designated area.

Native pollinators evolved with native plants, and many of them depend on the food and habitats that these plants provide. Eliminating pesticides and other chemicals benefits pollinators and other wildlife, encourages natural pest control, and protects watersheds and creeks. Integrated pest management methods can be effective for maintaining a natural balance rather than using chemicals that can harm beneficial insects. Most native plants do not require much fertilizer, which also contributes to the pollution of streams and water systems. Replacing conventional lawns with drought-tolerant native grasses further reduces the demand for irrigation, fertilizers, pesticides, and mowing.

By using low-impact maintenance practices, gardeners will help conserve natural resources, reduce waste, and protect the environment. More information on the subject can be found in *The Conscientious Gardener: Cultivating a Garden Ethic*, by Sarah Hayden Reichard.

## Water and Drainage

Water and drainage must be considered together because too much water and poorly drained soils are the most frequent causes of failure in the culture of native plants. Most natives may be watered freely during their periods of active growth, provided there is good drainage. Less irrigation is required if planting is done at the beginning of the rainy months, except in drought years when plants need supplemental irrigation in winter. Occasional summer irrigation may suit some of the adaptable natives and improve their appearance.

Sandy or gravelly, fast-draining soils require more frequent irrigation than clay soils composed of fine particles that retain moisture. For some natives, unaccustomed amounts of water tend to cause leggy growth and too much foliage at the expense of flowers. Occasional deep watering, rather than light sprinkling, is recommended for most plants to encourage deep rooting. As a rule, newly planted natives need supplemental irrigation for the first two or three summers to become established. Plants that are native to wet meadows, bogs, stream banks, or foggy regions may be watered throughout the year.

Drought-tolerant plants are accustomed to no water beyond that provided by the rains. Observation of plants in the wild in dry years shows that most species accept drought cycles without permanent damage, although there can be wilting or an early dormant period. Dormancy, often preceded by leaf drop, is a state of reduced activity that enables a plant to survive conditions of drought, cold, or other stress. Summer dormancy is an exacting requirement of many bulbs, corms, and deep-rooted plants. For these plants, no summer water should be given.

For best results, plants should be grouped according to their water requirements, and irrigation should be adjusted according to the season and the age of the plants. Watering on cooler days or in the early morning or evening reduces evaporation. Using an automated system can lead to excessive watering unless it is carefully monitored, and young plants in need of supplemental irrigation should be hand-watered. Drip irrigation is an efficient way to direct water to where it is needed, and it is useful on slopes to reduce runoff and erosion.

## Soil

The soils in California are diverse and complex. They include silt, sandy loam, clay, adobe, and conglomerates. Most California soils are neutral to alkaline, and they are often low in organic content. Some are rocky and infertile, while those of woodlands and forests may be mildly acid and more friable. Practically all soils will benefit from incorporating organic materials. The addition of such materials makes the soil easier to work, adds beneficial nutrients, and aids in water retention. Clay and adobe soils have a high water-holding capacity with poor drainage and aeration, and they should be worked when slightly moist.

Most native plants do not seem to have an absolute soil preference, with the exception of plants that grow in bogs, in serpentine areas, or in decomposed volcanic rock. Many plants adapted to serpentine soils can also grow in other soil types. Planting in raised beds or mounds improves the drainage for plants that often fail in heavy soils. Containers also provide good drainage, although they require more frequent watering. Clustering containers on a patio or near an entry can simplify watering, especially during the warm summer months when they need to be watered more often.

## Mulch

Covering the soil with a layer of mulch helps cool the soil, conserve moisture, and suppress weeds. It also gives a more finished appearance to a garden. Organic mulch, such as leaf litter and wood chips, adds nutrients to the soil as it decomposes and improves the soil structure. A three-inch layer of mulch is ideal, keeping it away from root crowns, and it can be replenished as needed. A light layer of inorganic mulch, consisting of gravel or crushed rock, is useful for rock gardens, around succulents, and for some container plantings.

## Weed Control

In addition to using mulch to discourage weeds, pulling out weed seedlings is preferable to using herbicides. Most weeds sprout in autumn with the first rains and again in early spring as the days become warmer. Large areas of annual weeds can be mowed, ideally before they produce seeds. The number of weeds usually decreases as gardens become established and plants grow to fill in the open spaces. Some plants introduced from other regions, as well as a few California natives, have become invasive and a threat to native vegetation. The California Invasive Plant Council publishes a list of native alternatives to invasive, exotic species and recommends landscaping with locally native plants adjacent to natural lands and preserves.

## Pest and Disease Control

Native plants are subject to the same sorts of pests and diseases that affect all plants. The idea persists that natives are more prone to disease when brought into gardens, but in my experience a healthy plant, grown with respect for its requirements, is seldom susceptible. Many problems can be avoided by providing appropriate irrigation, drainage, exposure, and space for plants to develop. Pests can generally be controlled by making the garden a habitat for beneficial insects and other wildlife rather than using chemical controls that may upset the natural balance.

## Pruning

Pruning benefits native plants by creating a good structure and enhancing aesthetic appeal. For some plants, pruning and shaping begins the first year to remove damaged, crowded, or crossing branches. Proper pruning can lower future maintenance costs. It can also reduce the risk of damage from insects and diseases by supporting healthy growth. As a rule of thumb, no more than twenty-five percent of a tree canopy or foliage should be removed each year. Coppicing is a method of pruning that involves cutting plants to the ground to encourage new growth. For large, old trees, such as established oaks, it is best to use a certified arborist for major pruning.

The pruning needs of trees and shrubs vary by species and growth habit. Most natives, including oaks and chaparral shrubs, should be pruned during their dormant period. Certain evergreen shrubs, especially ceanothus, are known to suffer dieback following the removal of large branches. Such removal should be done in dry weather because the chance of infection seems less. Some older plants, including coyote brush, mountain mahogany, Pacific wax myrtle, redbud, and toyon, respond to coppicing by producing vigorous new growth. These are some of the plants that resprout quickly after burning. Oaks, bays, maples, and redwoods will also produce new growth soon after cutting or fire. Cutting perennials back after flowering improves their form and sometimes stimulates a second bloom.

## Adaptability

An adaptable plant is able to accept conditions that vary from those of its natural habitat, such as more or less water, amounts of sun or shade, soils, and other factors. These are among the most reliable plants because they seem content with almost any garden situation. Some gardeners assume that all native plants are easy to grow and require no care. But when, for various reasons, they fail to perform as expected, gardeners often become discouraged and give up on them. Gardeners are more likely to be successful if they follow the cultural methods described here. A thoughtful selection of natives with suitable companions will produce a nearly self-sufficient California garden.

# PLANT DESCRIPTIONS

**THE PLANTS DESCRIBED** in the following chapters are reliable, attractive, available, and suitable for gardens in California's Mediterranean climate region. They are listed alphabetically by plant type: trees, shrubs, perennials, annuals, bulbs, vines, and grasses. The information given for each plant—name, distribution, size, and tolerances for exposure, water, and soil—will help gardeners make informed decisions about selecting and growing native plants.

Suggestions for companion plants are included together with wildlife value and traditional uses. Plants that prefer coastal or inland conditions are noted. Some of the most outstanding cultivars, of the numerous cultivars available, are described, and the choice of cultivars or species may depend on availability and the specific garden situation. Plants with similar garden requirements, and those noted for a special feature or specific garden use, are listed in the Plant Selection Guide.

## Plant Names

Each entry includes the scientific name, common name, and plant family. The only way to be certain of correctly identifying a plant is by its scientific name, which consists of two parts, the genus and the species. The generic name is capitalized, and the name designating the species, or specific epithet, is not.

The genus describes a group of related plants, and the species identifies the particular type of plant within the group. For example, the genus *Quercus* includes several species of oak, each with a specific designation, such as *Quercus agrifolia* for coast live oak.

Scientific names are in Latin or derived from other languages, generally Greek, or from the name of a place where the plant was found or the person who discovered or cultivated it. For example, *Eschscholzia californica*, was named in honor of Johann Friedrich von Eschscholtz, who collected the California poppy on a Russian expedition to San Francisco in 1816.

Common names can be misleading because some are used only locally, while others are used for more than one plant. A plant may have one or more common names that are often descriptive of its characteristics, such as coast live oak or pink-flowering currant. The most prevalent common names are used in this book.

A plant family is a grouping of plants with similar characteristics. The family name usually ends with the suffix *aceae*. Some plant families have only a few species, such as the walnut family (Juglandaceae), and others, like the sunflower family (Asteraceae), are represented by hundreds of species.

A cultivar or "cultivated variety" is a plant distinguished by certain preferred characteristics. When reproduced, the plant retains these characteristics. Cultivars are generally propagated vegetatively to preserve a particular trait, such as flower color or superior form. Cultivar names are non-Latin and enclosed in single quotation marks, as in *Arctostaphylos* 'Emerald Carpet'. Subspecies and variety are terms used to indicate some variation in form or structure.

## Distribution

Geographic distribution and plant communities or natural habitats in California are given for each plant. Plant communities are assemblages of plants that grow together because of similar adaptations to climate, soil, and terrain. They are generally named for the dominant plant or vegetation type, such as redwood forest, dominated by coast redwood, and chaparral, dominated by evergreen shrubs.

## Height and Spread

Average height and spread are given for each plant. Actual size varies according to microclimate, soil, horticultural practices, and age.

## Exposure

Sun and shade requirements are indicated, and plants should be grouped accordingly. Some plants that tolerate full sun in coastal regions will benefit from partial shade in inland gardens. Recommendations for sun exposure range from full sun to partial shade or shade.

## Water

Watering suggestions are for established plants during the dry months of the year. Few plants require irrigation in winter unless the rains are insufficient. Water requirements vary according to soils and microclimates. Plants should be grouped according to their irrigation needs, and watering schedules should be adjusted seasonally and as plants mature. Even drought-tolerant plants usually need supplemental irrigation until they become established.

**Drought tolerant:** Seasonal rainfall only
**Occasional:** Monthly
**Moderate:** 2–3 times per month
**Regular:** Weekly

## Soil

Many native plants are adaptable to various soil types, but some have specific preferences. It is best to select plants that are suited to the soils of the site. Drainage can be improved by mounding or amending heavy soils.

**Adaptable:** Plants that tolerate a range of soil types
**Heavy:** Plants that tolerate clay soil
**Well-drained:** Plants that prefer good drainage provided by sandy or rocky soils or slopes

## Abbreviations

**Cal.:** California
**co.:** county
**ft:** feet
**id., ids.:** island, islands
**in.:** inch
**mtn.:** mountain
**nor.:** northern
**pt.:** point
**so.:** southern
**sp., spp.:** species (sing. and pl.)
**ssp., sspp.:** subspecies
**var.:** variety

# TREES

Trees are the dominant and enduring feature of most landscapes. They occupy many habitats throughout California, from the windblown cypresses of coastal bluffs to the towering redwoods that thrive in fog-cooled canyons and mixed-evergreen and conifer forests in mountain regions. Oaks grow in coastal areas, in valleys, and in drier foothills with buckeyes and gray pines. Waterways support riparian woodlands composed of willows, maples, and other deciduous trees, some of which provide glorious fall color.

Trees have lasting value for gardens and landscapes. They provide shade, structure, and seasonal interest as well as food and shelter for wildlife. Their shade has the added effect of modifying the climate by lowering the air and ground temperatures beneath them on hot summer days. Most deciduous trees lose all of their leaves in the fall and produce a new set of leaves in early spring. They bring a seasonal effect and sunlight to the garden in autumn and winter, while evergreen species hold one or more sets of leaves throughout the year.

Conserving existing trees and planting desirable species of trees, thoughtfully selected from the many possibilities available, should be an early step for establishing a native garden. The selection of tree species should be made after evaluating the impact on the surrounding landscape. The most important traits to consider when choosing a tree are size, form, and growth rate. In some locations, the ultimate size of a tree may be limited by poor soils, lack of water, and strong winds. Ornamental characteristics to look for include unusual leaf forms or textures, distinctive bark patterns, cones, flowers, and fruits. The following species of native trees are some of my favorite selections. Native shrubs that have the potential to be used as small trees are listed in the Plant Selection Guide.

***Abies bracteata*** **Santa Lucia fir**

Pinaceae (Pine Family)

**Distribution:** Restricted to rocky slopes of the Santa Lucia Mountains in Monterey County up to 5,000 ft. **Height:** 75 ft. **Spread:** 15–20 ft. **Exposure:** Sun. **Water:** Drought-tolerant. **Soil:** Well-drained preferred.

Although Santa Lucia fir is one of the world's rarest firs, it is quite responsive to cultivation. It has a distinctive form with a narrow, spire-like crown, spreading lower branches, and lustrous dark green needles. Egg-shaped cones, held upright on the upper branches, are about four inches long with slender bracts exserted from cone scales. The growth rate is moderately rapid, about one foot or more a year. This tree is equally effective in small groves or planted as a single specimen in large gardens on north- or east-facing slopes. The Regional Parks Botanic garden has a mature grove of Santa Lucia firs, bearing abundant cones and seeds. The balsamic-resinous pitch from this fir was once used by Franciscan friars in religious ceremonies.

*Abies bracteata*, Santa Lucia fir

## *ACER* SPECIES (MAPLES)

Aceraceae (Maple Family)

Four species of maples are native to California, growing mostly near streams and in moist canyons of foothills and mountains. The seeds provide food for birds and squirrels, and the foliage is occasionally browsed by deer.

### *Acer circinatum* — Vine maple

**Distribution:** Shaded stream banks and coniferous forests in northern California. **Height:** 5–20 ft. **Spread:** 5–20 ft. **Exposure:** Sun or partial shade. **Water:** Moderate to occasional, when established. **Soil:** Adaptable.

Vine maple is a deciduous shrub or small tree with multiple trunks and a variable form that is sprawling and vine-like in shade or upright in open areas. Lobed leaves are medium green, turning red or orange in fall. Small reddish flowers in spring are followed by showy red samaras or winged seeds, and in winter the bare branches and pale gray bark are revealed. Vine maple has the delicacy of a Japanese maple and is ideal for small gardens, planted as a single specimen or in groves for a woodland effect. Ferns and Western bleeding heart are ideal companions. This tree requires some moisture and does best where leaf mold or other rich humus has been added to the soil. Although the growth rate is slow and plants seldom

*Acer circinatum*, vine maple

Vine maple, leaves and samaras

need pruning, they will accept pruning and training and can be grown in a large container. Vine maple is difficult to establish in southern California and inland valleys unless conditions of shade and moisture are met. I planted a grove of vine maples on the north side of my house in Lafayette, where they receive the maximum amount of shade, and they are lovely in every season of the year.

### *Acer macrophyllum* — Bigleaf maple

**Distribution:** Common on stream banks and in canyons and open woodlands below 5,000 ft. **Height:** 30–75 ft. **Spread:** 30–50 ft. **Exposure:** Sun or partial shade. **Water:** Moderate to occasional. **Soil:** Adaptable.

Bigleaf maple is a fast-growing and long-lived deciduous tree, providing year-round interest. In spring, its large, deeply lobed leaves emerge and are bright green to bronze. Pale green flowers appear at the same time and hang in pendant racemes. By September the foliage turns pale yellow in mild climates and a deeper color in mountain canyons. Clusters of samaras remain on the branches until autumn when they are carried away by the wind. Bigleaf maple is an excellent shade tree, and pruning is recommended to encourage the development of a broad, spreading crown. In Marjorie Schmidt's Los Gatos garden, a bigleaf maple planted at the edge

*Acer macrophyllum*, bigleaf maple

Bigleaf maple, fall color

of a lawn reached twenty-five feet in twelve years. Established trees require little summer water.

### *Acer negundo* — Box elder

This is a fast-growing deciduous tree that is widely distributed along streams throughout cismontane California from San Jacinto to Shasta County. Box elder is considered by some to be a weed tree which suckers and provides too many volunteers, but it can be useful for stabilizing stream banks. In my experience, it persists as a twenty- to thirty-foot tree for many years.

***Aesculus californica*** **California buckeye**

Hippocastanaceae (Buckeye Family)

**Distribution:** Common on dry slopes and canyons of the Coast Ranges and Sierra foothills, often growing with oaks, bays, and madrones. **Height:** 15–40 ft. **Spread:** 15–40 ft. **Exposure:** Sun. **Water:** Regular to drought-tolerant. **Soil:** Adaptable.

California buckeye is a fast-growing, broad-headed, deciduous tree or large shrub. The tracery of its bare branches and smooth, silver-gray bark are especially pleasing against a background of evergreen foliage through the fall and winter. Also of interest is the unfolding of leaf and flower buds in early spring. Bright green leaves have five to seven leaflets, and white or pale pink flower spikes attract many butterflies. Mid- to late-summer leaf drop is a drought adaptation. In autumn, heavy, pear-shaped fruits split open to reveal smooth, mahogany-brown seeds that sprout easily in moist soil, generally producing a number of seedlings at the base of the parent tree. Indians crushed the poisonous seeds and used them to stupefy fish, and the seeds were edible after roasting and leaching. Buckeye grows quickly from a deep tap root, and young plants need protection from deer until they grow above the browse line. It will grow rapidly, as much as two feet a year, with irrigation. Buckeye will also accept considerable dryness, but this leads to slower growth. Over time, some inner branches can be removed to eventually form an open, widely spreading tree. Coast live

*Aesculus californica*, California buckeye

California buckeye, fall-winter

oaks and buckeyes are good companions in a large garden, where their rounded forms and seasonal changes can be admired.

---

### *Alnus rhombifolia* — White alder

Betulaceae (Birch Family)

**Distribution:** Widely distributed along water courses and in meadows throughout California's foothills.
**Height:** 40–60 ft. **Spread:** 20–40 ft.
**Exposure:** Sun or partial shade.
**Water:** Regular. **Soil:** Adaptable.

*Alnus rhombifolia*, white alder catkin

White alder is a useful and fast-growing deciduous tree that can reach twenty feet or more in about five years. Shallow roots have the potential to become invasive, and deep watering helps young trees develop a deep root system rather than shallow surface roots. The tree's outstanding feature is a fringe of long, golden-beige catkins in the winter months. It has pale gray bark, well-spaced branching, and toothed leaves with prominent veining. Alders may be planted as lawn trees or in groves with a carpet of wild ginger and alum root. They are short-lived, which is typical of many fast-growing trees.

---

***Arbutus menziesii*** **Madrone**

Ericaceae (Heath Family)

**Distribution:** Wooded slopes and ravines below 5,000 ft in mixed-evergreen forests and chaparral. More abundant in North Coast Ranges and the Sierra Nevada. **Height:** 20–100 ft. **Spread:** 15–75 ft. **Exposure:** Sun to partial shade. **Water:** Drought-tolerant to occasional. **Soil:** Well-drained.

*Arbutus menziesii*, madrone

Madrone is considered to be the most beautiful of California's broadleaf trees, and it should be preserved where it occurs naturally. It is seldom recommended for the average home garden, but it can be used in large estates and parks with a mixture of conifers and broadleaved trees. Evergreen and widely branched, madrone is noted for its smooth, reddish bark and clusters of white urn-shaped flowers that bloom from March to May. Dark green, leathery leaves are three to six inches long, and brilliant orange to red berries enliven woodlands and attract flocks of birds in autumn. Difficult to establish, it is best to start with a small plant that is about two feet tall and to provide some shade. Water deeply about once a month until the young plant is well established. After several attempts, I finally succeeded in growing a madrone by planting in the late fall, just as the rains were starting. Once established, madrones need little care. They have a moderate growth rate and may remain small trees in cultivation. The shedding of leaves throughout the year is less noticeable when they are planted in the background or with other trees and shrubs. Some large old specimens, known as council trees, were the meeting place of Indian tribes.

Madrone, leaves and berries

### *Calocedrus decurrens* — Incense cedar or red cedar

Cupressaceae (Cypress Family)

**Distribution:** Mixed evergreen and coniferous forests in mountain slopes and canyons from Baja California to Oregon. **Height:** 50–90 ft. **Spread:** 10–15 ft. at base. **Exposure:** Sun. **Water:** Drought-tolerant to occasional. **Soil:** Adaptable, well-drained preferred.

Incense cedar is a slender, evergreen tree with shredding, cinnamon-brown bark. Highly recommended for its pyramidal form, attractive appearance, and moderate growth rate, this tree is resistant to pests and tolerant of heat and poor soils. Its small cones mature in one season, and female cones resemble ducks' bills. Incense cedar may be used as a specimen tree or screen in large gardens and parks. It tolerates drought, but it will flourish with a deep watering once a month during the dry season. Young trees grow slowly, but they may grow at the rate of two feet a year when es-

*Calocedrus decurrens*, incense cedar or red cedar

tablished. This tree is a good alternative to coast redwood in hot, dry inland areas. It is useful for a large hedge, wind screen, or specimen tree. The aromatic wood has been used for shingles, lead pencils, and cedar chests.

---

***Chamaecyparis lawsoniana*** **Lawson cypress or Port Orford cedar**
Cupressaceae (Cypress Family)

**Distribution:** Moist slopes and canyons, coastal and mixed evergreen forests of northern California. **Height:** 60 ft. **Spread:** 20 ft. **Exposure:** Partial shade. **Water:** Moderate. **Soil:** Adaptable.

Lawson cypress is an evergreen tree with full, pendulous lower branches and a narrow pyramidal top. It has scale-like, dark blue-green foliage and small brown cones that mature in autumn. Mature trees produce an abundance of cones, which are very decorative, on the lower branches. Roots need to be kept cool, or the tree can be lost suddenly to rhizoctonia rot. Best suited to mild climates, Lawson cypress is a superb specimen tree in coastal areas. It is recommended as a windbreak or screen and can be sheared as a hedge. Its attractive foliage and natural symmetry make Lawson cypress an excellent specimen tree.

*Chamaecyparis lawsoniana*, Lawson cypress or Port Orford cedar

**CULTIVARS** 'Ellwoodii' grows to eight feet tall, and 'Wisselii' reaches a height of eighteen feet with an irregular growth habit. 'Lutea' features golden leaves and grows to thirty feet or more.

## *CUPRESSUS* SPECIES (CYPRESSES)

Cupressaceae (Cypress Family)

Ten species of *Cupressus* are native to California, including the iconic Monterey cypress adapted to coastal sites of the Monterey Peninsula and Tecate cypress found on dry slopes of southern California.

### *Cupressus macrocarpa* — Monterey cypress

**Distribution:** Exposed headlands, Monterey Peninsula. **Height:** 40–80 ft. **Spread:** 40–80 ft. **Exposure:** Sun. **Water:** Drought-tolerant. **Soil:** Adaptable.

Monterey cypress is a beautiful evergreen tree that is pyramidal with a straight trunk when young, becoming broad and gnarled with age. Subject to canker fungus away from the coast, this fast-growing tree is useful in a cool, foggy climate. It is suitable for windbreaks and hedges.

*Cupressus macrocarpa*, Monterey cypress

***Cupressus forbesii*** **Tecate cypress**

**Distribution:** Dry slopes in chaparral in the Peninsular Ranges of southern California. **Height:** 15–30 ft. **Spread:** 20 ft. **Exposure:** Sun. **Water:** Drought-tolerant. **Soil:** Adaptable.

Tecate cypress is a small, fast-growing evergreen tree or large shrub with fire-adapted closed cones. Peeling, mottled brown and gray bark is an attractive feature. This tree is recommended for small gardens in hot, inland areas where it forms a slender and often irregularly branched specimen, sometimes remaining shrub-like. It is useful for screens and windbreaks and may be sheared to create a dense hedge. Cypress canker can be a problem, and overwatering makes this species more susceptible to infections. Once established, this cypress endures wind, heat, dryness, and hard soils.

***Juglans californica*** **California black walnut**

Juglandaceae (Walnut Family)

California has one species of walnut with two varieties: *Juglans californica* var. *californica* (southern black walnut) grows in coastal canyons of southern California and *Juglans californica* var. *hindsii* (northern black walnut) is found along streams.

***Juglans californica* var. *hindsii*** **Northern black walnut**

**Distribution:** Limited distribution along creeks in central California. **Height:** 30–60 ft. **Spread:** 30–60 ft. **Exposure:** Sun. **Water:** Drought-tolerant. **Soil:** Adaptable.

California walnut is a deciduous tree with wind-pollinated catkins and pinnately compound leaves that turn yellow in fall. It is widely used as a vigorous rootstock for English walnut. Indians used the nuts for food and

*Juglans californica*, California black walnut

planted them throughout the Coast Ranges and Sierra foothills. This tree provides food and cover for birds and squirrels. Yerba buena and snowberry have naturalized under an old walnut tree growing near the creek in my garden.

---

### *Lyonothamnus floribundus* — Catalina ironwood

Rosaceae (Rose Family)

**Distribution:** Dry slopes and chaparral, Catalina Island. **Height:** 20–50 ft. **Spread:** 15–20 ft. **Exposure:** Sun to partial shade. **Water:** Occasional to moderate. **Soil:** Adaptable.

Catalina ironwood is a slender, evergreen tree with compound leaves and large, creamy terminal flower clusters in spring or summer. Old flowers turn brown and persist for several years. Its gray to red-brown bark peels off in long thin strips, and new twigs are often reddish. This island endemic benefits from occasional irrigation in inland areas. Catalina ironwood is effective planted as a single specimen or in small groves with summer holly or manzanitas. The hard wood was used by Indians for spears, and settlers used the wood for making canes and fishing poles.

*Lyonothamnus floribundus*, Catalina ironwood

### ***Lyonothamnus floribundus* spp. *asplenifolius*** **Fernleaf ironwood**

This is considered to be an exceptionally handsome tree. It is similar is all respects to the species except for the foliage. Its leaves are divided into three to seven deeply notched or lobed leaflets, and it may be shrub-like with several trunks. Native to Santa Cruz, Santa Rosa, and San Clemente islands, this tree is widely planted in coastal areas. Ironwoods will tolerate light frost, but neither this variety nor the species is tolerant of prolonged freezing. Both are both fast-growing and accept pruning and shaping. Old trees can be cut to the ground to encourage new growth. The ironwoods are considered to be relict endemics, but fortunately they are available to gardeners.

## *PINUS* SPECIES (PINES)

Pinaceae (Pine Family)

Nineteen species of pine are native to California, and several are quite rare because of restricted distribution. A number of pines grow in foothills and mountain forests, and some are native to coastal areas. Many species are adaptable to cultivation and valuable for their symmetrical habit through all stages of their development. Low-elevation pines are the most popular for gardens and large-scale landscaping because they are relatively fast-growing and retain a balanced form. Pines are attractive planted as single specimens or in groves, with consideration given to growth rate and ultimate size.

Rates of growth vary from about six inches to two feet a year, with the height generally less than it is in the wild. Pines prefer lean and well-drained soil, and many species are drought-tolerant. They may be watered occasionally, but deeply, during the first two summers after planting. They seldom require pruning except for removal of dead wood. Tip growth or limbs may be cut when necessary, or the trees may be trained for some specific garden purpose.

Pines afford a dramatic accent to the garden and provide filtered shade in maturity. Gray pine (*P. sabiniana*), a natural companion to oaks and buckeyes, has handsome foliage and a wispy, open crown. Torrey pine (*P.*

*Pinus contorta*, beach pine

*Pinus radiata*, Monterey pine

*Pinus sabiniana*, gray pine

Gray pine, needles and cones

*Pinus torreyana*, Torrey pine

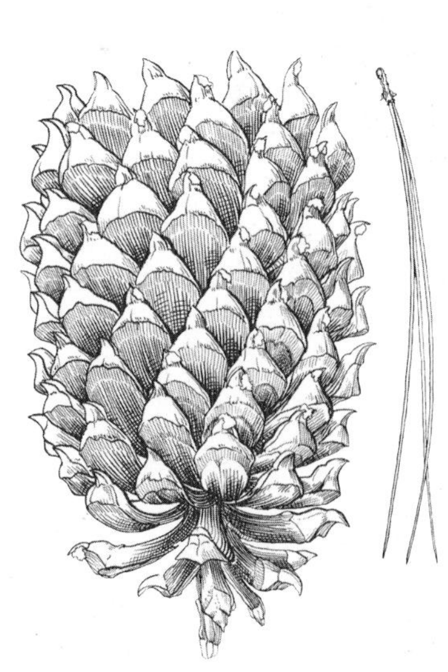

*Pinus coulteri*, Coulter pine

**TABLE 1.** *Pinus* (Pines)

| Plant | Distribution | Height | Spread |
|---|---|---|---|
| *P. contorta* (beach pine), plate | Coastal strand, Nor. Cal. | 10–35 ft | 10–35 ft |
| *P. coulteri* (Coulter pine), figure | Dry, rocky slopes, Coast Ranges, Mt. Diablo to Baja | 30–75 ft | 24–40 ft |
| *P. radiata* (Monterey pine), plate | Central Coast | 80–100 ft | 25–35 ft |
| *P. sabiniana* (gray pine), plates | Dry foothills, Coast Ranges and Sierra Nevada | 40–80 ft | 30–50 ft |
| *P. torreyana* (Torrey pine), plate | San Diego Co. and Santa Rosa Id., rare | 40–60 ft | 30–50 ft |

*torreyana*) is rare in the wild, and it attains larger proportions in gardens than in its native habitat. Beach pine (*P. contorta*) is suitable for coastal gardens or containers. Monterey pine (*P. radiata*), widely planted as a fast-growing tree, is not recommended for most residential areas because it is short-lived, flammable, and susceptible to pests and diseases.

Pine nuts were a nutritious food for the California Indians, and they still use pine needles for making decorative baskets. The trees provide shelter for wildlife, and many birds and animals feed on their seeds.

### ***Platanus racemosa*** — **California sycamore**

Platanaceae (Sycamore Family)

**Distribution:** Riparian areas of the Coast Ranges. **Height:** 30–80 ft. **Spread:** 20–50 ft. **Exposure:** Sun. **Water:** Occasional to moderate. **Soil:** Adaptable.

California sycamore is a large, stately tree with mottled bark and large, maple-like leaves. It is impressive growing along waterways and seasonal streams, especially in winter when the branches are bare and the pale bark can be admired. Fall foliage color is yellow to brown, and ball-shaped seeds persist on bare branches through the winter. This tree is susceptible to anthracnose or sycamore blight, which causes leaf drop in cool, moist conditions. Suitable for large gardens, California sycamore is a fast-growing and long-lived tree with single or multiple trunks.

| Cones | Culture | Comments |
|---|---|---|
| 1-2 in. cones | Regular water, good in containers | Best near coast, fast growth |
| Long, oval, closed cones | Tolerates drought, heat, and wind | Moderate growth rate, good screen |
| 3-6 in. cones | Occasional water | Very fast growth, short-lived, shallow roots, diseases |
| 6-10 in. cones | Drought-tolerant, coastal or inland areas | Fast growth, open crown, gray-green foliage |
| 4-6 in. cones | Tolerates drought, heat, and wind | Fast growth, adaptable, broad crown |

*Platanus racemosa*, California sycamore

### *Populus fremontii* — Fremont cottonwood

Salicaceae (Willow Family)

**Distribution:** Widely distributed along rivers and streams in valleys, canyons, and foothills below 6,500 ft. **Height:** 40–60 ft. **Spread:** 30 ft. **Exposure:** Sun. **Water:** Moderate to regular. **Soil:** Adaptable.

Fremont cottonwood is a fast-growing deciduous tree that is suited to inland regions. Glossy, yellow-green leaves, triangular in shape and coarsely toothed, turn bright yellow in fall. Catkins appear in spring before the leaves open, and female trees produce masses of cottony seeds that blow around. The bark is pale gray and deeply fissured. This tree has aggressive surface roots and is best kept away from drain pipes and pavement. Freemont cottonwood is ideal for watercourses and stream banks. 'Nevada' is a male cultivar with good form.

*Populus fremontii*, Fremont cottonwood

---

***Pseudotsuga menziesii*** **Douglas fir**

Pinaceae (Pine Family)

**Distribution:** Moist slopes and mixed forests, below 5,000 ft elevation, coastal regions from Monterey County north and from Fresno County north and eastward in the Sierra Nevada. **Height:** 70–150 ft in cultivation. **Spread:** 20–30 ft. **Exposure:** Sun to partial shade. **Soil:** Adaptable. **Water:** Occasional to regular.

Its dense, pyramidal form makes Douglas fir a popular Christmas tree. Deep green or blue-green, fragrant needles radiate in all directions around the branches, and reddish-brown cones are pendulous, with thin scales and protruding, three-pronged bracts. Trees are moderately fast-growing and retain their pyramidal form for many years until they lose their lower branches, with age. Douglas fir does best in its home territory or in similar conditions.

## *QUERCUS* SPECIES (OAKS)

Fagaceae (Oak or Beech Family)

California has twenty species of native oaks, most with sturdy, often rugged trunks, and wide-spread branching. Oaks are a pleasing aspect of valleys, foothills, and mountains. They are widely distributed and occur at many elevations from near the coast to the Sierra Nevada. Oak trees have been traditionally revered for their majestic form. Valley oak was probably the one most frequently mentioned in early literature, and it can still be seen in parklike groves in a few areas. It is also considered to be among the most adaptable and water tolerant of the native oaks. Coast live oak (*Q. agrifolia*), blue oak (*Q. douglasii*), and Engelmann oak (*Q. engelmannii*) are typically found in arid foothills.

Oaks vary in size from shrubby forms to large trees with spreading branches. Evergreen or deciduous leaves vary from oval to broadly elliptic, some with lobes and others with serrated or entire margins, and of firm or leathery texture. Flowers occur in spring catkins; the slender and pendulous male catkins are conspicuous because of the yellow stamens that release clouds of pollen to the wind, and the female ones are solitary and less showy. Acorns vary in size by species and mature in late summer and fall.

All oaks are easily grown from acorns, and growth rate is moderate. Trees grown from acorns often surpass nursery-grown trees in size and vigor. Many acorns are planted by jays and squirrels, and it is best to remove unwanted seedlings before their taproots become developed.

*Quercus agrifolia*, coast live oak

**TABLE 2.** *Quercus* (Oaks)

| Plant | Distribution | Height | Spread |
|---|---|---|---|
| *Q. agrifolia* (coast live oak), plate | Valleys and Coast Ranges, Sonoma to San Diego | 35–70 ft | 35–70 ft |
| *Q. douglasii* (blue oak), plate | Dry interior valleys, central and So. Cal. | 30–50 ft | 40–70 ft |
| *Q. engelmannii* (Engelmann oak) | Dry valleys, So. Cal. | 40–50 ft | 40–50 ft |
| *Q. kelloggii* (California black oak), plate | Foothills, woodlands and forests | 30–80 ft | 30–80 ft |
| *Q. lobata* (valley oak), plates | Valleys, foothills, riparian areas | 40–100 ft | 40–100 ft |

Some pruning may be necessary during the early years of growth to remove crossing limbs and lower branches. Stumps will sprout after pruning or fire.

Occasional deep watering encourages deep rooting in young oaks, but summer irrigation should be avoided around mature trees to prevent root problems. Good drainage is essential to prevent crown rot or root fungus, and lawns and other groundcovers that require summer water are not recommended for planting under oaks. Pathogens that affect oaks include

*Quercus douglasii*, blue oak

| Foliage | Culture | Comments |
|---|---|---|
| Evergreen, dark green | Drought-tolerant | Shade tree, rounded form, wildlife value |
| Deciduous, lobed leaves | Drought-tolerant | Fall color, slow growth |
| Deciduous, blue-green | Drought-tolerant | Open crown |
| Deciduous, lobed leaves | Drought-tolerant | Shade tree, plant with conifers |
| Deciduous, lobed leaves | Prefers deep soil, water-tolerant with drainage | Adaptable, fast growth, graceful form |

oak root fungus (*Armillaria mellea*) and crown rots (*Phytophthora* spp.). *Phytophthora ramorum* causes sudden oak death (SOD), which is threatening oaks in central and northern California.

There is increasing interest in oaks, and they are protected trees in many communities. Tragically, many established oaks die in or near construction sites for the following reasons: poor soil drainage, lack of air circulation around roots because of compacted soil, grading too near the trunks, and changes in natural soil level because of grading. When a

*Quercus kelloggii*, California black oak, leaves

*Quercus lobata*, valley oak

*Quercus lobata*, Valley oak, leaves

change in grade or soil level is necessary, retaining walls or dry wells may be constructed to keep the original soil line intact.

Oaks are beautiful, long-lived trees for gardens and parks, planted as specimens or in groves for a woodland effect. Although no one can expect to see a fully developed oak grove in his or her lifetime, a well-proportioned tree can be had in ten to fifteen years. Once established, oaks can produce several feet of new growth each year. Plants that tolerate dry shade are good companions, and oak leaf litter should remain on the ground as mulch.

Acorns were the primary food source for tribes throughout California, and indigenous communities were often based on the distribution of oak groves. Oaks and their acorns are important to wildlife, especially in winter when other foods are scarce. Birds and small animals find food and shelter among their branches, and deer eat the acorns in autumn to fatten up for the lean winter months.

## ***Sequoia sempervirens*** **Coast redwood**

Taxodiaceae (Taxodium Family)

**Distribution:** Coast Ranges from Central California to southern Oregon in the coastal fog belt, mostly below 2,000 ft. **Height:** 70–100 ft. **Spread:** 15–30 ft. **Exposure:** Sun to partial shade. **Soil:** Adaptable. **Water:** Occasional to moderate.

Towering forests of coast redwood along the California coast are a compelling sight. Growing up to three hundred and fifty feet in the wild, coast redwood is the world's tallest tree, and some specimens are more than two thousand years old. Redwoods have reddish-brown bark, small brown cones, and flattish, sharp-pointed needles, forming sprays of evergreen foliage on horizontal or drooping branches. The foliage has a distinctive, pungent fragrance, which is especially noticeable on foggy days. All phases of the coast redwood's growth are attractive, especially in spring when new growth appears like delicate scalloping edging the foliage sprays.

*Sequoia sempervirens*, coast redwood

Young trees grow rapidly, as much as three to five feet a year with regular watering, and less under semi-dry conditions. Sun is acceptable in coastal areas, but shelter and a thick layer of mulch should be provided inland or where drying winds prevail. Trees often looked stressed with inadequate moisture on hot, dry sites, and they do not tolerate freezing temperatures at elevations higher than their normal range. Redwoods are generally pest-free.

Coast redwoods are suitable for large gardens or parks, planted singly or in groves with ferns, wild ginger, pink-flowering currant, and Pacific wax myrtle. Redwoods can also be pruned as hedges. The decay-resistant wood is used for houses, fences, and decks. Several selections are available with desirable characteristics such as dense and uniform growth habit, and foliage color that varies from wild forms.

**CULTIVARS** 'Aptos Blue' has attractive blue-green foliage on horizontal branches with drooping branchlets; 'Soquel' has dark green needles on horizontal branches with turned-up tips.

### *Sequoiadendron giganteum* — Giant sequoia

This tree is closely related to the coast redwood and notable for its massive size. It grows in isolated groves on west slopes of the Sierra Nevada and tolerates a greater range of altitude and temperature than the coast redwood. Trees are often troubled by *Botryosphaeria* blight, especially when crowded. Giant sequoia is suited to colder inland areas and performs best in large-scale plantings where it can reach one hundred feet or more in height with a spread of thirty to fifty feet.

---

### *Thuja plicata* — Western red cedar

Cupressaceae (Cypress Family)

**Distribution:** Moist forests from coastal northern California. **Height:** 50–100 ft. **Spread:** 25–60 ft. **Exposure:** Sun or partial shade. **Water:** Occasional to regular. **Soil:** Adaptable.

*Thuja plicata*, Western red cedar

Growing up to two hundred feet in the wild, western red cedar is a magnificent tree with a symmetrical form and broadly spreading branches. It has flat sprays of small, scale-like leaves and small, brown cones. This tree is ideal for parks and lawns, and it can be pruned as a hedge or screen.

**CULTIVARS** 'Collyer's Gold' is a compact form that grows slowly to six feet. New growth is yellow, and interior foliage is green. 'Emerald Clone' is a selection with bright green foliage that grows up to eighty feet tall.

## *Torreya californica* **California nutmeg**

Taxaceae (Yew Family)

**Distribution:** Scattered groves in cool, shaded canyons below 4,500 ft. **Height:** 15–20 ft. **Spread:** 10–15 ft. **Exposure:** Sun or partial shade. **Water:** Moderate. **Soil:** Adaptable.

California nutmeg is a handsome, slow-growing conifer with an open pyramidal crown and horizontal branches. The seed cone has a plum-like wrapping that turns from pale green to purple in fall. Sharp-pointed, two- to four-inch dark green needles were used for tattooing by the California Indians.

*Torreya californica*, California nutmeg

## *Umbellularia californica* **California bay**

Lauraceae (Laurel Family)

**Distribution:** Common in canyons and valleys below 5,000 ft, woods and forests of several plant communities, Coast Ranges and Sierra Nevada from San Diego County to southwest Oregon. **Height:** 25–50 ft. **Spread:** 25–50 ft. **Exposure:** Sun or shade. **Water:** Drought-tolerant to moderate. **Soil:** Adaptable.

California bay is a slow-growing evergreen tree with pungent, aromatic foliage. It grows to seventy-five feet in moist woodlands and is shrublike in windy coastal areas. Trees may

*Umbellularia californica*, California bay

be single- or multi-trunked, and the trunks will sprout after pruning or fire. Clusters of small yellow flowers are followed by purple olive-like fruits that are not edible. The seeds should be planted fresh and will eventually sprout. Although California bay has few problems with pests and diseases, it is known to be one of the host plants for the pathogen that causes sudden oak death. California bay trees are useful in large-scale gardens, where they give shade and enhance other plantings. They are also suitable as hedges or windbreaks, or they can be clipped into various shapes for a formal garden. A few, which have attained tremendous size, are held in high esteem and have been protected in some communities. The leaves are used to season food, and the hard wood is used to make a variety of artifacts.

# SHRUBS

Shrubs are woody plants with multiple trunks or branches from the base, ranging in size from low groundcovers to about fifteen feet or the height of a small tree. California has a wide variety of native shrubs, and some are entirely indigenous to the state. Chaparral vegetation is dominated by drought-tolerant, evergreen shrubs, and shrubs adapted to moist places can be found in forests and woodlands. Ceanothus and manzanitas are among the most admired native shrubs, comprising two of the state's major groups of woody plants.

Creative combinations of deciduous and evergreen shrubs add variety and seasonal interest to many garden settings. Together with trees, shrubs provide a durable framework for the native garden. They can be used as focal points, with perennials and grasses, or to provide a background for other plants. Shrubs are also useful for hedges, screens, and erosion control. Some of the most important traits to consider when making a selection are colors and textures of foliage, flowers, fruits, and bark.

## *Adenostoma fasciculatum* **Chamise**

Rosaceae (Rose Family)

**Distribution:** Chaparral in foothills of the Coast Ranges and Sierra Nevada.
**Height:** 3–10 ft. **Spread:** 3–10 ft. **Exposure:** Sun. **Water:** Drought-tolerant.
**Soil:** Adaptable, well-drained preferred.

Chamise is a tough, dense shrub, characteristic of chaparral vegetation, that tolerates heat and drought. Its name is derived from the fascicled (clustered) leaves that remain on the plant all year. It has short needlelike leaves with small, white flower clusters appearing on the ends of branches from late spring into summer. This deep-rooted and long-lived shrub is useful on slopes for erosion control, and a prostrate form makes an attractive groundcover. Chamise is highly flammable and should be kept away from structures. After a fire the plants will reestablish themselves by crown-sprouting. Chamise is a source of nectar for butterflies.

**CULTIVARS** 'Santa Cruz Island' has deep, green foliage and a mounding habit, growing two feet tall with a four-foot spread. It thrives in a sunny, well-drained site with little or no summer water. 'Nicolas', from San Nicolas Island, is a prostrate selection that spreads up to six feet.

*Adenostoma fasciculatum*, chamise, low form

## *ARCTOSTAPHYLOS* SPECIES (MANZANITAS)
Ericaceae (Heath Family)

California is home to fifty-seven species of *Arctostaphylos,* and more than one hundred named cultivars have been introduced. This genus is notable for horticultural possibilities and for natural hybrids that occur where several species overlap. Members of this genus are commonly called *manzanita*, Spanish for little apple, because of the shape of the fruits. Manzanitas, together with ceanothus, are emblematic of the California landscape and recognized for their many attributes. They are attractive in every season, and many species, especially some of the larger ones, become more beautiful with age.

Manzanita, flowers

Although widely distributed throughout the state and found in many habitats, most species are native to dry places. They

Manzanita, bark

Manzanita, berries

often occur in almost unbroken masses in chaparral and dry foothills. Some species make dense carpets on coastal bluffs and others grow in the Sierra Nevada up to 10,000 feet elevation. One species, bearberry or kinnikinnick (*A. uva-ursi*), is circumpolar.

Manzanitas are among the most handsome, enduring, and useful of all native shrubs, with exceptional value for gardens and landscapes. They are evergreen, woody shrubs of uniform growth habit that range in size from low, creeping or mounding plants to large shrubs with tree-like proportions. Some species are suitable for massed plantings, and others can stand alone as garden accents. In spite of their reputation for having crooked branches, many have open and arching branches that are well-spaced for a pleasing outline.

Manzanita, leaves

Manzanitas are especially noted for their sculptural trunks and smooth, mahogany-colored bark, which peels in late spring or early summer at the end of the growing season.

Some, like Pajaro manzanita (*A. pajaroensis*), have fibrous, reddish-brown bark. Manzanitas have distinctive drought-adapted, evergreen leaves that are generally held vertically on the stems. Leaves are firm and leathery, ranging in color from pale or bright gray-green to darker shades of green, and some have a blue cast. A nice contrast is afforded by new leaves that emerge in late winter, which are generally pale and occasionally red or bronze.

*Arctostaphylos edmundsii*, Little Sur manzanita

Some species start to bloom in October or November, and others flower through the winter months into early spring. Small, fragrant, urn-shaped flowers are borne in terminal racemes or panicles, and they vary only slightly in size among the species. Flower colors include white, pale to deep pink, and rose; those with large clusters often have a waxy appearance. The flowers are an important winter source of nectar for hummingbirds, and edible, red berries are enjoyed by a variety of birds and animals in late summer and fall.

Once established, many manzanitas are easy to grow, thriving with sun or light shade, little or no irrigation, and occasional pruning to shape or

*Arctostaphylos manzanita* 'Dr. Hurd', Dr. Hurd manzanita

**TABLE 3A.** *Arctostaphylos* (Manzanitas), Low Shrubs and Groundcovers

| Plant | Distribution | Height | Spread |
|---|---|---|---|
| *A. edmundsii* (Little Sur manzanita),[a] plate | Coastal bluffs, Monterey area, rare | 12 in. | Up to 12 ft |
| *A.* 'Emerald Carpet', plate | Cultivar, hybrid of *A. uva-ursi, A. nummularia* | 8–14 in. | 5 ft |
| A. *hookeri* (Hooker manzanita)[b] | Monterey Bay area | 3 ft | 4–8 ft |
| *A.* 'John Dourley' | Cultivar | 2–3 ft | 6 ft |
| *A.* 'Pacific Mist' | Cultivar | 2–3 ft | 6–10 ft |
| *A. pumila* (sandmat manzanita) | Coastal dunes, Monterey area | 12 in. | 6 ft |
| *A. nummularia* (Ft. Bragg manzanita)[c] | Coast, Sonoma to Mendocino | 12 in. | 1–2 ft |
| *A. uva-ursi* (bearberry[d]) | Central Coast, Sierra Nevada | 1 ft | 6–12 ft |

[a]*A. edmundsii* Cultivars: 'Bert Johnson' is mat-forming with gray-green leaves and white flowers. 'Carmel Sur' has gray-green leaves, a spreading habit, and tolerates garden conditions. Both selections are best in coastal areas.

[b]*A. hookeri* Cultivar: 'Monterey Carpet', is a low, spreading selection, and 'Wayside' forms low mounds.

[c]*A. nummularia* Cultivar: 'Small Change' is a mounding form with shiny, deep green leaves and small white flowers.

[d]*A. uva-ursi* Cultivars: 'Point Reyes' has dark, leathery leaves and a trailing form. It does best in coastal areas. 'Radiant' is fast-growing with bright green leaves, and 'Woods Red' has dark green leaves and large, red berries. All are useful on slopes and for spilling over walls.

remove dead branches. Red galls along the leaf edges of young leaves are produced by manzanita leaf fold aphids (*Tamalia coweni*) that live inside the galls, typically on new growth. They are harmless and can be removed by cutting back the affected leaves or the leaves will die and fall off after the aphids leave the galls. A unique trait of some species is the ability to stump-sprout after a fire and eventually develop a heavy, basal, burl-like root. Others depend upon seed for their regeneration.

The berries were used by Indians and early settlers for a pleasant-tasting cider, and household items were fashioned from the hard wood. The generic name, which means "bear-grape," comes from bears' fondness for the berries. Indians and trappers ground the leaves of some manzanitas with those of other shrubs as a substitute for smoking tobacco, known as kinnikinnik, another common name for the genus. A delicate honey is produced from the flowers.

| Flowers | Culture | Comments |
|---|---|---|
| Soft pink | Sun, tolerates moisture and heavy soil | Groundcover, good form and foliage |
| Pale pink | Sun in coastal areas, inland shade and moisture | Uniform groundcover, attractive foliage |
| White | Sun, semi-dry | Dense mounds, good on slopes |
| Pink-tinged white | Sun, tolerates irrigation | Blue-green foliage, reddish new growth |
| Pinkish white, sparse bloom | Sun, drought-tolerant, best inland | Gray-green leaves, good on slopes |
| White | Sun, water or drought | Adaptable, tolerates heavy soils |
| White, small | Light shade, acid soil | Shiny leaves, rock garden with conifers |
| White or pink | Inland shade | Good under trees |

*Arctostaphylos* 'Emerald Carpet', emerald carpet manzanita

**TABLE 3B.** *Arctostaphylos* (Manzanitas), Medium to Tall Shrubs

| Plant | Distribution | Height | Spread |
|---|---|---|---|
| *A. bakeri* 'Louis Edmunds', plate | Cultivar, selected in 1950s | 5–8 ft | 5–6 ft |
| *A. densiflora* 'Howard McMinn' | Cultivar, widely planted | 4–6+ ft | 4–6 ft |
| *A. densiflora* 'Sentinel' | Cultivar | 6–8 ft | 4–10 ft |
| *A. glauca* (bigberry manzanita) | Chaparral, Coast Ranges, So. Cal. | 10–15 ft | 10–15 ft |
| *A. insularis* (island manzanita) | Chaparral, Santa Cruz and Santa Rosa Ids. | 10–12 ft | 10–12 ft |
| *A.* 'Lester Rowntree' | Hybrid of *A. obispoensis, A. pajaroensis* | 8 ft | 8 ft |
| *A. manzanita* 'Dr. Hurd', plate | Cultivar | 10–15 ft | 10–15 ft |
| *A. pajaroensis* (Pajaro manzanita),[a] plate | Central Monterey Bay | 4–8 ft | 10–12 ft |
| *A.* 'Sunset'[b] | Hybrid of *A. hookeri* and *A. pajaroensis* | 4–5 ft | 4–5 ft |

[a]*A. pajaroensis* Cultivars: 'Paradise' has an open, spreading form, gray-green leaves, and large flower clusters. 'Warren Roberts' is an outstanding selection with blue-green leaves and good garden performance. On both selections, the new foliage has a reddish-bronze color and fades to green.

[b]Cultivar: *A.* 'Sunset' is a garden-tolerant cultivar that was named for *Sunset* magazine's 75th anniversary.

*Arctostaphylos bakeri* 'Louis Edmunds', Louis Edmunds manzanita

| Flowers | Culture | Comments |
|---|---|---|
| Pink | Sun, tolerates irrigation and clay soils | Reliable, gray-green leaves, upright form |
| Rose pink | Sun, tolerates clay soils, adaptable | Reliable, fine-textured green leaves, round form |
| Rose pink | Sun, adaptable | Upright, open branching, gray-green leaves |
| Pink to white, abundant | Sun, dry, well-drained soil | Best inland, blue-gray leaves |
| White | Sun, moderate water, tolerant of clay soils | Bright green leaves; erect form |
| Pink | Sun, monthly irrigation, well-drained soil | Refined, blue-green foliage |
| White | Sun, tolerates some irrigation | Best inland, tree-like, large leaves |
| Pink to white | Sun, drought-tolerant | Shredding bark, new leaves reddish-bronze |
| Pink to white | Sun, drought-tolerant | Dense foliage |

*Arctostaphylos pajaroensis* 'Paradise', Pajaro manzanita

### *Artemisia californica* — California sagebrush

Asteraceae (Sunflower Family)

**Distribution:** Coastal scrub and chaparral throughout California. **Height:** 2–4 ft. **Spread:** 3–6 ft. **Exposure:** Sun. **Water:** Drought-tolerant to occasional. **Soil:** Adaptable.

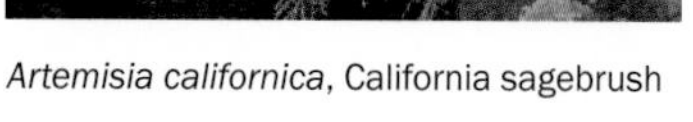

*Artemisia californica*, California sagebrush

California sagebrush stands out for its soft, silver-gray foliage. Leaves are fine-textured with a pleasant, pungent aroma. This plant looks best with light pruning to stimulate new growth. Occasional deep watering will improve its appearance in summer. California sagebrush is attractive combined with sages, monkeyflowers, and buckwheats on a sunny slope.

**CULTIVARS** 'Canyon Gray' grows to about one foot in height and spreads up to ten feet. 'Montara' forms a mound up to three feet tall and five feet wide. Both are excellent prostrate selections with pleasing, silvery foliage.

### *Artemisia douglasiana* — Mugwort

This plant grows rapidly to six feet in height and spreads by rhizomes in moist, shady areas. Its serrated leaves are dark green above with silver undersides. Stems should be cut to the ground in fall to stimulate new growth. This species is a good choice for seeps and other naturally moist places.

### *Artimesia pycnocephala* 'David's Choice' — David's Choice sandhill sagebrush

This is a superb, compact selection of sandhill sagebrush with silver-gray leaves. It forms low mounds and is best in coastal gardens. Removing flower heads in late summer helps maintain its attractive appearance and form.

*Artemisia pycnocephala*, sandhill sagebrush

---

**_Baccharis pilularis_** **Coyote brush**

Asteraceae (Sunflower Family)

**Distribution:** Coastal scrub and chaparral along the coast from Russian River to Monterey County. **Height:** 1–2 ft for coastal forms. **Spread:** 4–6 ft. **Exposure:** Sun. **Water:** Drought-tolerant to moderate. **Soil:** Adaptable.

Coyote brush is a tough, evergreen shrub that tolerates heat, wind, and poor soil. It performs admirably in sandy and heavy soils and is suitable for coastal and inland sites. Cutting the plants back every few years is recommended to improve their appearance, and some of my plants are still vigorous after thirty years as a result of periodic pruning. They are generally available in flats and usually reach their mature size in a year or two. Propagation by cuttings perpetuates plants having the best features and foliage color. Male plants are usually cultivated for landscaping because female plants produce abundant seeds and have weedy potential, especially in disturbed areas. Coyote brush is an important habitat plant, providing food and cover for birds, butterflies, and small animals.

**CULTIVARS** 'Twin Peaks' and 'Pigeon Point' are male selections with low, spreading habits, ideal for erosion control on sunny slopes. Both are fast-growing, long-lived, and fire-resistant with occasional irrigation. 'Twin Peaks' has small dark green leaves, and 'Pigeon Point' has larger leaves that are lighter green.

*Baccharis pilularis*, coyote brush, low form

## *BERBERIS* SPECIES (BARBERRIES)

Berberidaceae (Barberry Family)

These handsome evergreen shrubs have holly-like leaves, brilliant yellow flower clusters, and colorful fruits. They have also been classified as *Mahonia*. Leaves are pinnately compound and range in color from dark green to gray-green. The berries attract birds, and the foliage provides refuge and nesting sites. Pruning is helpful to shape and control size, and cutting back or removing old, woody canes encourages new growth. Barberries are useful for foundation plantings, hedges, and barriers. The roots have been used for making a yellow dye for baskets and fabrics.

### *Berberis aquifolium* — Oregon grape

**Distribution:** Wooded slopes of mountain forests in northern California and Oregon. **Height:** 4–6 ft. **Spread:** 3–4 ft. **Exposure:** Sun to shade. **Water:** Occasional to moderate. **Soil:** Adaptable.

The year-round attributes of this attractive shrub are undisputed. Glossy, dark green leaves are pinnate with three, five, or seven leaflets with spines on the margins. New growth in spring is reddish-bronze, and leaves turn a deep red or bronze in winter. Bright yellow flower clusters in spring are followed by glaucus, blue berries in late summer and fall. Oregon grape has long been a popular garden plant. It is most handsome in part shade,

*Berberis aquifolium*, Oregon grape

as a foundation planting on the cool side of buildings, or in a mixture of trees and shrubs. It thrives with some leaf mold in the soil and performs better with some shade in hot, inland areas.

**CULTIVAR** *Berberis aquifolium* 'Compacta' grows to a height of two to three feet, spreading by rhizomes to five feet or more. Plants produce few flowers, but they are useful as groundcovers. They can be cut back occasionally to promote denser growth and maintain a uniform height.

### *Berberis nervosa* — Longleaf barberry

Longleaf barberry is a vigorous plant that resembles a large, leathery fern. It forms colonies in damp woodlands of northern Coast Ranges and requires shade except on the northern coast. This species is generally slow to become established in gardens.

### *Berberis nevinii* — Nevin's barberry

**Distribution:** Coastal sage scrub and chaparral in southern California. **Height:** 6 ft. **Spread:** 6 ft. **Exposure:** Sun. **Water:** Drought-tolerant to occasional. **Soil:** Adaptable.

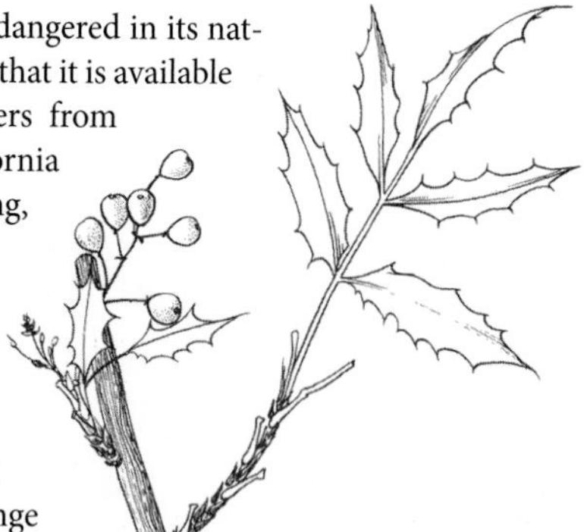

This barberry is rare and endangered in its natural habitat so it is fortunate that it is available as a garden plant. Gardeners from central to southern California consider it to be an enduring, evergreen shrub with excellent year-round appearance. The attributes of this barberry include blue-green leaves with yellow-gold flower clusters in spring, followed by red-orange berries that mature in summer. Nevin's barberry is relatively slow-growing and tolerates porous or heavy soils. It is effective in a dry garden with sages and native grasses.

**_Berberis pinnata_** **California holly grape**

California holly grape is similar to Oregon grape, but the leaves are more wavy and prickly. Native to coastal scrub, chaparral, and woodland, this species tolerates dry conditions in sun or shade.

**CULTIVAR** *Berberis* 'Golden Abundance' is a hybrid selection, aptly named for its abundant flower clusters. It spreads by rhizomes to form a dense thicket up to eight feet tall and makes a good hedge or screen.

**_Berberis repens_** **Creeping barberry**

This species has a low, spreading form and matte, rather than glossy, green leaves. It is a reliable ground and slope cover in full sun or part shade with little or no irrigation.

## ***Calycanthus occidentalis*** **Spice bush**

Calycanthaceae (Sweet-Shrub Family)

**Distribution:** Moist places, such as canyons and streams in the northern Coast Ranges and Sierra Nevada. **Height:** 5–8 ft. **Spread:** 5–8 ft. **Exposure:** Sun to partial shade. **Water:** Occasional to regular. **Soil:** Adaptable.

This large, deciduous shrub has long been a garden favorite for its rounded form, dense habit, large aromatic leaves, and unusual, maroon-colored flowers. The flowers have been described as having the scent of strawberries or old wine. Plants are in bloom between April and August, and decorative woody fruits persist into winter after the leaves have fallen. With regular water, spice bush is a fast-growing shrub that tolerates full sun near the coast and light shade inland. It is effective with ferns and sedges in a woodland garden or as an informal hedge or screen. Experiences at botanic gardens show it to be long-lived.

*Calycanthus occidentalis*, spice bush

Spice bush, flower

***Carpenteria californica*** **Bush anemone**

Philadelphaceae (Mock Orange Family)

**Distribution:** Restricted range in Sierra foothills of Fresno County. **Height:** 4–6 ft. **Spread:** 4–6 ft. **Exposure:** Sun to partial shade. **Water:** Drought-tolerant to occasional. **Soil:** Adaptable.

*Carpenteria californica*, bush anemone

Bush anemone is a handsome evergreen shrub, long admired by gardeners on the West Coast and in Europe for its lovely flowers. Terminal clusters of white, anemone-like flowers with yellow stamens appear in early spring. This shrub tolerates full sun near the coast and prefers afternoon shade inland. The dark green leaves and shredding bark have a shabby appearance in late summer, and that is the best time to cut plants back by up to two-thirds to promote new growth. The many uses for this lovely shrub include planting it as a specimen or with a mixture of trees and shrubs. It combines well with currants and irises among oaks or conifers.

**CULTIVAR** 'Elizabeth', a selection made by Wayne Roderick, has a compact form with dense flower clusters.

## *CEANOTHUS* SPECIES (CEANOTHUS OR WILD LILACS)

Rhamnaceae (Buckthorn Family)

This large and diverse genus, found only in North America, has about sixty species and varieties in California. Members grow in several plant communities, but their greatest concentration is in foothill regions. Like manzanitas, ceanothus range in size from mat-forming or low mounding forms to large, tree-like shrubs, with most being medium-sized shrubs of dense to rangy outline. With few exceptions, they are evergreen with spectacular flowers, and all need full sun for good bloom.

Early plant explorers were attracted to these blue-flowered shrubs, and several species were grown in Europe in the 18th century. Others were developed in French and Belgian nurseries, of which the well-known *Ceanothus* 'Gloire de Versailles' is one of the most popular. There was little interest in California until the 20th century, except for a few species such as blue blossom (*C. thyrsiflorus*), when several botanists and horticulturalists studied ceanothus and disseminated seeds and information. Their popularity has increased with the selection of superior hybrids and the introduction of new cultivars. Further refinement continues, along with studies in adaptability and uses. Variable traits within the genus, added to the frequency of natural hybrids, leads to the assumption that this genus is still evolving, and we can look forward to new possibilities.

Many species have graceful, spreading branches, and some are noted for their pale, smooth bark. Leaves tend to be small to medium in size,

*Ceanothus griseus horizontalis*, Carmel creeper

*Ceanothus hearstiorum*, Hearst ceanothus

*Ceanothus maritimus*, maritime ceanothus

**TABLE 4A.** *Ceanothus* (Ceanothus), Low Shrubs and Groundcovers

| Plant | Distribution | Height | Spread |
|---|---|---|---|
| *C.* 'Centennial' | Cultivar | 2 ft | 5 ft |
| *C. gloriosus* (Pt. Reyes ceanothus)[a] | Coastal bluffs, Pt. Reyes to Mendocino | 1–3 ft | 8–12 ft |
| *C. gloriosus* var. *porrectus* (Mt. Vision ceanothus) | Woods, Marin Co., rare | 1–2 ft | 4–6 ft |
| *C. gloriosus exaltatus* ('Emily Brown') | Cultivar | 3–4 ft | 8 ft |
| *C. griseus horizontalis* (Carmel creeper),[b] plate | Coastal, Santa Barbara to Mendocino | 1–3 ft | 4 ft |
| *C. hearstiorum* (Hearst ceanothus), plate | Rare, near Hearst Castle | 6–12 in. | 6 ft |
| *C.* 'Joyce Coulter' | Hybrid | 3 ft | 10–12 ft |
| *C. maritimus* (maritime ceanothus),[c] plate | Rare endemic, near Hearst Castle | 1–3 ft | 3–8 ft |

[a]*C. gloriosus* Cultivars: 'Anchor Bay' has deep blue flowers and spreads to six feet. 'Heart's Desire' is a low, spreading form with pale blue flowers. Both are excellent, adaptable groundcovers for coastal gardens.

[b]*C. griseus* Cultivar: 'Yankee Point' is a fast-growing, dependable groundcover with glossy, dark green leaves and medium blue flowers, useful for coastal and inland areas.

[c]*C. maritimus* Cultivars: 'Frosty Dawn' spreads slowly to six feet and features dark blue flowers. It performs best near coast with well-drained soil. 'Pt. Sierra' has smaller leaves, arching branches, and tolerates inland heat with some shade.

from less than one inch up to three inches in Catalina ceanothus (*C. arboreus*). Some are rough-textured and others are smooth, while a few are thick and glossy with undulate and spiny margins. Leaf color varies from dark green to yellow-green and many shades in between, and foliage is attractive throughout the year.

Ceanothus is known for dazzling floral displays, with flowers appearing from February to June. Individually, the flowers are small, fragrant, and abundant in panicles or racemes. The inflorescence varies with each species, and it may consist of short, dense clusters or large, compound spikes of feathery beauty. Flower color ranges through many shades of blue to purple, white, and occasionally pink. Fruits are rounded capsules that split open in summer to release their seeds.

Members of this genus are among California's prime drought-tolerant shrubs. Most species are drought-tolerant and prefer full sun and well-drained soil. They often grow in poor soil on steep, south-facing

| Flowers | Culture | Comments |
|---|---|---|
| Violet-blue, short clusters | Some shade inland | Small, shiny leaves |
| Light blue, 1 in. clusters | Sun, inland shade, some moisture | Dark green 1 in. leaves |
| Violet-blue | Tolerates shade and some water | Small, holly-like leaves |
| Dark violet-blue | Tolerates heavy soil, some water | Dark green, 1 in. holly-like leaves |
| Light blue, 1 in. clusters | Adaptable to coast or inland | Glossy, green leaves, bank cover |
| Light to deep blue | Sun near coast, inland shade | Low mat, short-lived well-drained soil |
| Medium blue | Tolerates heavy soil and water | Medium green leaves, forms dense mound |
| White to pale lavender | Adaptable, partial shade inland | Blue-green leaves, gray undersides |

*Ceanothus arboreus*, Catalina ceanothus

*Ceanothus impressus*, Santa Barbara ceanothus

**TABLE 4B.** *Ceanothus* (Ceanothus), Medium to Tall Shrubs

| Plant | Distribution | Height | Spread |
|---|---|---|---|
| *C. arboreus* (Catalina ceanothus),[a] plate | Brushy slopes, Channel Ids | 12–20 ft | 15–20 ft |
| *C.* 'Blue Jeans' | Cultivar | 8–10 ft | 8–10 ft |
| *C.* 'Concha' | Cultivar | 6–8 ft | 6–8 ft |
| *C.* 'Dark Star' | Cultivar | 6 ft | 6 ft |
| *C.* 'Frosty Blue' | Cultivar | 8–12 ft | 8–12 ft |
| *C. griseus* 'Louis Edmunds' | Cultivar | 4–6 ft | 12–15 ft |
| *C. impressus* (Santa Barbara ceanothus), plate, figure | Chaparral, Central Coast | 6–9 ft | 10–15 ft |
| *C.* 'Julia Phelps' | Cultivar, widely planted | 4–7 ft | 7–9 ft |
| *C.* 'Ray Hartman' | Hybrid of *C. arboreus, C. grisseus* | 12–18 ft | 15–20 ft |
| *C.* 'Sierra Blue' | Cultivar | 10–15 ft | 10–15 ft |
| *C. thyrsiflorus* (blue blossom),[b] plate | Chaparral and woodlands, Coast Ranges | 6–20 ft | 6–20 ft |

[a]*C. arboreus* Cultivar: 'Cliff Schmidt', an upright selection from Santa Cruz Island, has medium blue flowers and large, felted leaves. In coastal areas, it blooms in spring and again in fall.

[b]*C. thyrsiflorus* Cultivars: 'El Dorado' is a variegated selection that grows to eight feet with an equal spread, featuring dark green leaves with yellow highlights. 'Skylark' grows three to six feet tall, spreading to six feet, with dark blue flower clusters and emerald-green leaves. 'Snow Flurry' is a large, fast-growing shrub with glossy green leaves and white flowers.

slopes, and many have nitrogen-fixing bacteria in nodules on their roots. Plants generally require little care, but shaping, tip-pruning, and removing interior dead wood can improve their appearance. Late summer and fall are the best time for pruning. Once established, they require little or no irrigation.

There seems to be a ceanothus for every situation, except perhaps the shady, well-watered garden. The prostrate types are useful as groundcovers on slopes or spilling over walls. Low-growing species generally perform best near the coast, and they are useful for erosion control on slopes. Medium to large shrubs can be used as background plantings, screens, or

| Flowers | Culture | Comments |
|---|---|---|
| Lavender blue | Sun, semi-dry | Dull green leaves, white undersides |
| Pale, powder blue | Tolerates heavy soil and water | Small, dark green leaves |
| Dark blue, 1 in. clusters | Tolerates summer water, reliable | Dark green 1 in. leaves, arching habit |
| Dark cobalt blue | Tolerates summer water | Dark green ¼ in. leaves, reliable |
| Deep blue, frosted white | Adaptable | Dark green ½ in. leaves |
| Bright blue | Sun, semi-dry, adaptable | Glossy green 1 in. leaves, fast-growing |
| Dark blue, 1 in. clusters | Best near coast | Dark green 1 in. leaves |
| Dark indigo, 1 in. clusters | Adaptable, well-drained soil | Dark green ½ in. leaves, reliable |
| Medium blue | Adaptable | Dark green 2–3 in. leaves, reliable |
| Medium blue, 8 in. clusters | Full sun near coast or inland | Glossy, medium green 1½ in. leaves |
| Light to dark blue | Adaptable | Glossy green 2 in. leaves, fast-growing |

*Ceanothus impressus*, Santa Barbara ceanothus

*Ceanothus thyrsiflorus*, blue blossom

accents. As a mass planting, they are spectacular during their spring flowering season. In the wild, entire hillsides are illuminated with a blue haze when ceanothus is flowering.

Longevity varies by species; some live only six to ten years, and others may persist for more than twenty years with infrequent irrigation and well-drained soils. Annual pruning of new growth is recommended for most species to improve their appearance. Their relatively short life span is an adaptation to periodic fires in California's coastal scrub and chaparral plant communities. Most are fast-growing and easy to replace in gardens. Many species and cultivars are available in nurseries, all outstanding for their form, abundance of flowers, and excellence of leaf texture or color.

Ceanothus has habitat value for birds, butterflies, and small animals. Deer tend to browse species with large leaves and generally avoid eating those with small, spiny leaves. Traditionally the flowers have been used as a soap substitute.

***Cercis occidentalis*** **Western redbud**

Fabaceae (Pea Family)

**Distribution:** Dry slopes and canyons in foothills below 4,500 ft of the inner Coast Ranges, Peninsular Ranges, and Sierra Nevada. **Height:** 6–18 ft. **Spread:** 10 ft. **Exposure:** Sun to partial shade. **Water:** Drought-tolerant to occasional. **Soil:** Adaptable, well-drained preferred.

Western redbud provides garden interest in every season, from the magenta-colored flowers and heart-shaped leaves that emerge in early spring, to the cinnamon-brown seed pods in autumn, and the winter framework of smooth, reddish-brown trunks. Leaves turn yellow in fall, and seed pods persist through the winter on bare branches. Redbud is long-lived and blooms more profusely with each passing year. It may be pruned to suit its situation, and some of the trunks may be removed to form a small, open tree. Redbud is effective with an underplanting of Sonoma sage or combined with evergreen shrubs, such as ceanothus and coffeeberry. California Indians coppiced the plant to produce straight new stems for basketry.

*Cercis occidentalis*, Western redbud

***Cercocarpus betuloides*** **Mountain mahogany**

Rosaceae (Rose Family)

**Distribution:** Common on dry slopes and foothills below 6,000 ft in cismontane California. **Height:** 5–20 ft. **Spread:** 5–6 ft. **Exposure:** Sun. **Water:** Drought-tolerant to occasional. **Soil:** Adaptable.

Mountain mahogany is a large, evergreen shrub or small tree with an upright habit, arching branches, and smooth, silver-gray bark. Its small, birch-like leaves have a pinnate vein pattern on the upper surface. Small ivory flowers are seldom noticed, but the slender, silver, feathery seeds or achenes are striking when backlit by the sun. This long-lived shrub is fast-growing with occasional water, and basal shoots are easily removed. Old plants can be cut back to the base to promote new growth and restore their attractive form. Mountain mahogany contrasts nicely with toyon and ceanothus. It merits greater use in gardens as a specimen, screen, or background plant for its refined appearance and year-round interest. Native Americans used the hard wood for arrow tips, digging sticks, and fishing spears, and a pipe was made from the root.

---

***Cneoridium dumosum*** **Bushrue or berryrue**

Rutaceae (Rue Family)

**Distribution:** Bluffs and mesas in coastal sage scrub and chaparral, southern California. **Height:** 3–5 ft. **Spread:** 5 ft. **Exposure:** Sun to partial shade. **Water:** Drought-tolerant to moderate. **Soil:** Adaptable.

Noted for its aromatic foliage, this evergreen, compact shrub has small, white, solitary or clustered flowers that begin blooming in winter after a heavy rain and continue into spring. Foliage resembling mistletoe leaves is strongly scented from glandular dots on the lower surface. Fruits are globose berries, yellow-pink, aging to crimson, and brown when ripe with one or two dark brown seeds. Bushrue is considered to be a neat and charming shrub, little cultivated outside its native habitat. Plants need sun for most of the day when growing near the coast and some shade in warmer interior regions. This small shrub was persistent at Rancho Santa Ana Botanic Garden, where it provided many volunteers.

## *Comarostaphylis diversifolia* **Summer holly**

Ericaceae (Heath Family)

**Distribution:** Dry slopes and chaparral in coastal southern California. **Height:** 6–18 ft. **Spread:** 6–18 ft. **Exposure:** Sun to partial shade. **Water:** Drought-tolerant to occasional. **Soil:** Adaptable, well-drained preferred.

*Comarostaphylis diversifolia*, summer holly

Summer holly is an adaptable and enduring large shrub, outstanding for its evergreen foliage and colorful red fruits, similar to those of madrone. Dark green leaves have serrated margins and tomentose undersides. White, urn-shaped flowers in long, terminal racemes appear in spring, and the fruits attract birds from August to October. Mature shrubs have a dense, rounded habit and are equally effective as massed plantings or single specimens. The Regional Parks Botanic Garden has a large summer holly that produces a wealth of berries each autumn.

*Comarostaphylis sericea*, Summer holly, berries

***Cornus sericea*** **Creek dogwood or redtwig dogwood**

Cornaceae (Dogwood Family)

**Distribution:** Moist places and coniferous forests in northern California. **Height:** 7–9 ft. **Spread:** to 12 ft or more. **Exposure:** Sun or shade. **Water:** Occasional to regular. **Soil:** Adaptable.

Creek dogwood is a deciduous shrub that is grown for its red winter twigs. It spreads rapidly by rhizomes and rooting branches to make thickets that provide cover for wildlife. Small, cream-colored flowers bloom throughout the summer, followed by white or bluish fruits that attract many kinds of birds. Foliage turns soft yellow or red in autumn. Creek dogwood is suitable for creek banks and may be combined with plants with similar requirements, such as snowberry and hazelnut. Native Americans used its vibrant red stems for basketry.

*Cornus sericea*, creek dogwood or redtwig dogwood

## *Corylus cornuta* var. *californica* — California hazelnut

Betulaceae (Birch Family)

**Distribution:** Damp places in the northern Coast Ranges and Sierra Nevada. **Height:** 6–12 ft. **Spread:** 6–12 ft. **Exposure:** Sun or partial shade. **Water:** Occasional to moderate. **Soil:** Adaptable.

California hazelnut is a spreading, deciduous shrub that bears edible nuts, although they are seldom abundant. The rounded, green leaves are coarsely toothed and enhanced by soft hairs. Leaves turn bright yellow in autumn. The main attraction comes in winter when the male catkins begin to form, gradually elongating into elegant, golden-beige tassels. California hazelnut is lovely with irises and spring-flowering bulbs. Under garden conditions of shade and water, California hazelnut tends to become a large, many-stemmed shrub. The nuts are relished by small animals and birds.

*Corylus cornuta* var. *californica*, California hazelnut

## *DENDROMECON* SPECIES (BUSH POPPIES)

Papaveraceae (Poppy Family)

Two species of *Dendromecon* are native to California. Important plants of chaparral and foothill regions, they are noted for their displays of bright yellow flowers. Ceanothus, manzanitas, sages, buckwheats, and other drought-tolerant natives make good companions.

### *Dendromecon harfordii* — Island bush poppy

**Distribution:** Dry slopes in chaparral on the Channel Islands. **Height:** 8–20 ft. **Spread:** 8–20 ft. **Exposure:** Sun. **Water:** Drought-tolerant. **Soil:** Well-drained.

Island bush poppy is larger than its mainland relative. Its long season of bloom, from April to July and intermittently through the year, give this shrub high ornamental value. After flowering it can be pruned to shape. It should be given room to reach its full size.

### *Dendromecon rigida* — Bush poppy

**Distribution:** Common in dry slopes and chaparral at lower elevations in the Coast Ranges and Sierra Nevada. **Height:** 4–8 ft. **Spread:** 4–6 ft. **Exposure:** Sun. **Water:** Drought-tolerant. **Soil:** Well-drained.

Bush poppy can be long-lived when its requirements for heat and dryness are met. This unique poppy has a pleasing aspect with its open and rounded habit, smooth, gray-green leaves, and long succession of glowing, yellow flowers in spring. Companion plants include other chaparral shrubs and grasses.

*Dendromecon rigida*, bush poppy

### *ERIOGONUM* SPECIES (BUCKWHEATS)
Polygonaceae (Buckwheat Family)

Several species of buckwheats are woody perennials that might be classified as shrubs, including Santa Cruz Island buckwheat (*E. arborescens*), flat-topped buckwheat (*E. fasciculatum*), and St. Catherine's lace (*E. giganteum*). See the Perennials chapter for a description of these and other species of *Eriogonum*.

### ***Fremontodendron californicum*** — **Fremontia or flannel bush**
Malvaceae (Mallow Family)

**Distribution:** Scattered stands in chaparral; foothills of Sierra Nevada from Shasta County to San Diego County. **Height:** 6–15 ft. **Spread:** 12 ft. **Exposure:** Sun. **Water:** Drought-tolerant. **Soil:** Well-drained.

One of the most colorful plants named for John C. Fremont, fremontia is a large, evergreen shrub, stiff in appearance, with a profusion of bright yellow flowers from March to July. Dry conditions and full sun are essential for this species to thrive in gardens. Plants are susceptible to a canker-like disease in moist conditions. Fremontia is a fast-growing, short-lived shrub that needs room to spread. Its dark green felted foliage affords a sharp

*Fremontodendron californicum*, Fremontia or flannel bush

contrast with trees and shrubs, but gardeners should avoid contact with its irritating hairs. It is striking when used as a single specimen in a large garden, where its showy yellow flowers can be admired, or combined with one of the blue-flowered ceanothus.

***Fremontodendron decumbens*** **Pine Hill fremontia**

Pine Hill fremontia has a low, spreading habit and yellow-orange flowers. It can be difficult to grow in gardens. 'El Dorado Gold', a hybrid, is more garden-tolerant with a mounding form and yellow-orange flowers.

***Fremontodendron mexicanum*** **Mexican fremontia**

This species is similar to *F. californicum* with yellow-orange flowers and a longer season of bloom.

**CULTIVARS** 'California Glory' is a tree-sized shrub that bears an abundance of large, clear yellow flowers. 'Pacific Sunset' is an outstanding hybrid that grows to thirty feet in height and produces yellow-orange flowers.

---

## *Galvezia speciosa* Island snapdragon

Scrophylariaceae (Figwort Family)

**Distribution:** Coastal scrub below 3,000 ft on San Clemente and Santa Catalina islands. **Height:** 3–4 ft. **Spread:** 5–7 ft. **Exposure:** Sun to partial shade. **Water:** Drought-tolerant. **Soil:** Adaptable.

Scarlet, tubular flowers on this spreading shrub attract hummingbirds and resemble the nonnative, annual snapdragon. They bloom throughout the year, but most abundantly in spring. Adapted to island conditions, this shrub does not tolerate more than the occasional frost. Island snapdragon is useful on banks and benefits from pruning.

**CULTIVAR** 'Firecracker' is a compact selection with bright red flowers, growing to three feet with an equal spread.

*Galvezia speciosa*, island snapdragon

---

**_Garrya elliptica_** **Coast silk-tassel**

Garryaceae (Silk-Tassel Family)

**Distribution:** Dry slopes and ridges in chaparral and mixed evergreen forests in the Coast Ranges below 2,000 ft, from Ventura County to Oregon. **Height:** 8–12 ft. **Spread:** 10–20 ft. **Exposure:** Sun or partial shade. **Water:** Occasional. **Soil:** Adaptable.

Coast silk-tassel is a popular garden plant, highly valued for its decorative male catkins, which appear in December and remain in fine form until mid-spring. Clusters of slender, silver-gray tassels are outstanding against dark green, evergreen foliage. Female catkins produce six-inch clusters of grape-like fruits. This adaptable shrub may be grown as a specimen, pruned into a small tree, or used as an espalier against a wall. In hot inland gardens, coast silk-tassel requires some shade and supplemental irrigation.

**CULTIVARS** 'James Roof' is a selected male form with pendulous catkins a foot or more in length. It is a large shrub with an abundance of catkins fringing the entire plant. 'Evie' is also a large shrub with smaller leaves and slightly shorter catkins than 'James Roof'.

*Garrya elliptica*, coast silk-tassel

Coast silk-tassel, catkin

---

***Gaultheria shallon*** **Salal**

Ericaceae (Heath Family)

**Distribution:** Mixed evergreen and redwood forests, and coastal headlands from Santa Barbara north. **Height:** 1–8 ft. **Spread:** 2–10 ft. **Exposure:** Partial or full shade. **Water:** Regular .

Salal is a spreading, evergreen shrub that makes relatively rapid growth with shade, humus, acid soil, and moisture. It will also grow in dry conditions but much more slowly. Clusters of urn-shaped, white or pink flowers on terminal racemes bloom from March to June. Glossy, green leaves have serrate margins and a leathery texture. Where plants are sheared regularly, the reddish twigs and bronzy new foliage make an interesting contrast. This plant is most useful as a groundcover under redwoods, where it forms dense colonies from creeping roots, or in a shady border with ferns and wild ginger. Birds enjoy the dark purple fruits, and the Indians made the berries into a syrup.

*Gaultheria shallon*, salal

## *Hesperoyucca whipplei* — Our Lord's candle

Agavaceae (Agave Family)

**Distribution:** Chaparral in central and southern California. **Height:** 3 ft. **Spread:** 3 ft. **Exposure:** Sun. **Water:** Drought-tolerant. **Soil:** Well-drained.

Our Lord's candle forms a dense rosette of narrow gray-green leaves, up to two feet long, with toothed edges and needlelike tips. Large panicles of creamy white flowers bloom in profusion on spikes up to eight feet tall. Each plant blooms only once after ten to twenty years and dies after flowering, usually with a circle of new pups to take its place. Used as a single specimen or in groups, *Hesperoyucca whipplei* adds a sculptural element to a dry garden.

*Hesperoyucca whipplei*, Our Lord's candle

## *Heteromeles arbutifolia* **Toyon**

Rosaceae (Rose Family)

**Distribution:** Common in woodlands and chaparral below 4,000 ft in foothills of the Coast Ranges and Sierra Nevada. **Height:** 6–10 ft. **Spread:** 6–10 ft. **Exposure:** Sun to partial shade. **Water:** Drought-tolerant to occasional. **Soil:** Adaptable.

*Heteromeles arbutifolia*, toyon

Toyon's value to gardens is well-established as a reliable, evergreen shrub with a rounded crown and brilliant red berries in late autumn and winter. Named by the Ohlone tribe, toyon is the plant that gave Hollywood its name. If Californians ever decide to have an official state shrub, toyon would be a fitting candidate. It is widely cultivated, typical of foothill regions, and belongs almost exclusively to California. Toyon is mostly a dense shrub, but it tends to be rangy in wooded areas. It is amenable to pruning and may be grown as a large, multi-trunked shrub or trained as a small tree by gradual removal of lower limbs. Plants will stump-sprout after hard pruning or fire, and old plants can be cut back to the base to promote new growth and regain a dense form. Toyon is recommended as an accent plant, hedge, or background plant for drought-tolerant native shrubs and perennials. Birds feast on the berries, and they were gathered and eaten by many Indian tribes, after cooking them to remove the bitter taste. Early settlers made a ciderlike drink from the berries.

**CULTIVAR** 'Davis Gold' is a superb selection with orange berries.

**_Holodiscus discolor_** **Cream bush or ocean spray**

Rosaceae (Rose Family)

**Distribution:** Mixed evergreen and redwood forests of the Coast Ranges and Sierra Nevada. **Height:** 3–10 ft. **Spread:** 2–8 ft. **Exposure:** Partial shade. **Soil:** Adaptable. **Water:** Occasional to regular.

Cream bush is noted for its large sprays of creamy white flowers that enhance woodlands and shady gardens in late spring and early summer. It is equally attractive in its pre-blooming period with its many spires of pink-tinged flower buds. Leaves of this deciduous shrub are deeply grooved with serrate margins. Tolerant of moist and dry conditions, cream bush grows taller in moist, rich soil. Plants may be pruned to suit their garden situation, and spent flowers are easily removed.

*Holodiscus discolor*, cream bush or ocean spray

**_Keckiella antirrhinoides_** **Yellow bush penstemon**

This is a leafy shrub with showy, yellow flowers from the chaparral regions of southern California. It grows to six feet with an equal spread.

*Keckiella cordifolia*, heart-leaf keckiella

**Keckiella cordifolia** **Heart-leaf keckiella**
Scrophulariaceae (Figwort Family)

**Distribution:** Dry slopes and canyons in chaparral below 4,000 ft; San Luis Obispo County to Baja California and Channel Islands. **Height:** 3–6 ft. **Spread:** 3–6 ft. **Exposure:** Sun to partial shade. **Water:** Drought-tolerant to moderate. **Soil:** Adaptable, well-drained preferred.

Keckiellas are shrubby, drought-tolerant plants closely related to the genus *Penstemon*. *K. cordifolia* is a loosely branched, sometimes climbing, vigorous shrub with scarlet flowers that attract hummingbirds from late spring into early summer. It is summer-deciduous in hot, dry areas and semi-deciduous near the coast. Leaves are medium green with toothed margins. Cutting plants back when dormant will stimulate new growth in winter and spring. Heart-leaf keckiella typically grows up through chaparral shrubs, and suitable companions include coffeeberry, toyon, and ceanothus.

---

**Lavatera assurgentiflora** **Tree mallow**
Malvaceae (Mallow Family)

**Distribution:** Coastal scrub in Channel Islands and naturalized in coastal valleys. **Height:** 5–10 ft. **Spread:** 5–10 ft. **Exposure:** Sun to partial shade. **Water:** Drought-tolerant to occasional. **Soil:** Adaptable, well-drained preferred.

This fast-growing, short-lived shrub has large maplelike leaves and rose-purple flowers with prominent veins. Tree mallow can reach five to ten feet the first year from seed. It blooms from spring to fall and can be

*Lavatera assurgentiflora*, tree mallow

sheared after flowering. Plants need protection from gophers, rabbits, and deer. Tolerant of wind and salt spray, tree mallow is useful as an informal hedge for coastal gardens.

---

### *Myrica californica* — Pacific wax myrtle

Myricaceae (Wax Myrtle Family)

**Distribution:** Moist slopes and canyons in coastal California from the Santa Monica Mountains to Oregon. **Height:** 10–30 ft. **Spread:** 10–30 ft. **Exposure:** Sun to partial shade. **Water:** Occasional to regular. **Soil:** Adaptable.

*Myrica californica*, Pacific wax myrtle

Pacific wax myrtle is a large, evergreen shrub or small tree that is attractive throughout the year. It is admired for its handsome, dark green foliage and for its usefulness as a screen, clipped hedge, specimen, or background plant. The leaves have a spicy fragrance when crushed, and the purple, wax-coated berries attract birds.

Adapted to cool, coastal summers, this shrub requires some irrigation in inland gardens. In hotter areas plants are often troubled by spider mites, and thrips can be a problem near the coast. Pacific wax myrtle is amenable to pruning and shaping. Cutting plants back every few years promotes new growth and keeps them denser, and old shrubs can be cut back to re-sprout and regain a fuller form.

---

***Philadelphus lewisii*** **Western mock orange**

Philadelphaceae (Mock Orange Family)

**Distribution:** Slopes and canyons in chaparral and forests below 4,500 ft in northern California. **Height:** 4–10 ft. **Spread:** 6–12 ft. **Exposure:** Sun to partial shade. **Water:** Occasional to moderate. **Soil:** Adaptable.

An ideal choice for a lightly shaded garden, western mock orange is a lovely, deciduous shrub with arching branches and light green leaves. Dense

*Philadelphus lewisii*, Western mock orange

racemes of fragrant, white flowers perfume the air from late spring to early summer.

**CULTIVARS** *Philadelphus lewisii* spp. *californicus* 'Marjorie Schmidt' is an outstanding selection with larger flowers. Wild rose, snowberry, and creek dogwood are frequent companions. 'Goose Creek' is a choice cultivar with double flowers, and 'Covelo', a Suncrest Nursery selection, has single white flowers with yellow stamens.

---

### *Physocarpus capitatus* — Ninebark

Rosaceae (Rose Family)

**Distribution:** Moist slopes in many plant communities of the Coast Ranges and Sierra Nevada. **Height:** 6–8 ft. **Spread:** 6–8 ft. **Exposure:** Sun to partial shade. **Water:** Occasional to moderate. **Soil:** Adaptable.

Named for its peeling bark, ninebark is a deciduous, spirea-like shrub that is common along streams in many parts of California. Plants may be low and prettily disposed among boulders of mountain streams or taller in woodlands and forests. Clusters of small, white flowers appear in late spring, followed by red fruits. Bush anemone and Pacific wax myrtle are fitting companions for a north-facing slope.

**CULTIVAR** 'Tilden Park' is a prostrate form that makes a handsome groundcover, growing to about three feet tall and spreading widely.

*Physocarpus capitatus*, ninebark

## *PRUNUS* SPECIES (WILD CHERRIES)

Rosaceae (Rose Family)

The two species of wild cherries described here have evergreen, holly-like foliage, and edible fruits. They hybridize readily when grown together. Long-lived with a moderate growth rate, wild cherries are suitable for background planting, clipped hedges, and screens. The abundant flowers attract native pollinators as well as European honeybees, and the fruits are an important food source for birds and other wildlife.

### *Prunus ilicifolia* — Hollyleaf cherry

**Distribution:** Common in foothills of Coast Ranges and on Santa Catalina and San Clemente islands. **Height:** 10–25 ft. **Spread:** 10–25 ft. **Exposure:** Sun to partial shade. **Water:** Drought-tolerant to occasional. **Soil:** Adaptable.

Hollyleaf cherry has thick, glossy, bright green leaves with toothed margins. Racemes of white flowers in spring are followed by deep red fruits in fall. This versatile and reliable shrub has been in cultivation for over a hundred years. Seedlings appear in abundance and show a wide range of leaf types.

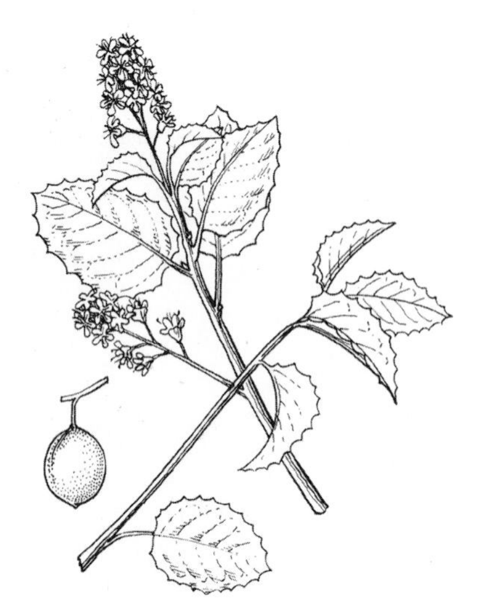

## *Prunus lyonii* — Catalina cherry

**Distribution:** Canyons and chaparral of the Channel Islands. **Height:** 15–20 ft. **Spread:** 15–20 ft. **Exposure:** Sun to partial shade. **Water:** Drought-tolerant to occasional. **Soil:** Adaptable.

Similar to hollyleaf cherry, Catalina cherry is always presentable as a single specimen or hedge. It can be grown as a multi-trunk shrub or trained as a small tree. Dark green leaves have smooth or undulate margins, and white flower spikes are followed by purple-black fruits. Fruit drop can be a nuisance when shrubs are grown near paved surfaces.

*Prunus lyonii*, Catalina cherry

## *RHAMNUS* SPECIES (COFFEEBERRIES OR BUCKTHORNS)

Rhamnaceae (Buckthorn Family)

This genus is known for evergreen shrubs of fine proportions, and for black fruits that give the name coffeeberry to most species. The decorative fruits transition from green through red to black when mature, and they attract birds and small mammals. Coffeeberries have a moderate growth rate and range in size from medium to large and sometimes spreading shrubs with presentable foliage. Several are notable for their prominently veined leaves, while others have glossy, dark green foliage. These shrubs are tolerant of pruning and shaping, and they combine well with ceanothus, manzanitas, and western redbud. Young plants make moderately rapid growth. This is a versatile genus with much to offer California gardeners.

**TABLE 5.** *Rhamnus* (Coffeeberries)

| Plant | Distribution | Height | Spread |
|---|---|---|---|
| *R. californica* (coffeeberry),[a] plate | Coastal Cal. | 3–15 ft | 8 ft |
| *R. crocea* (redberry), figure | Coastal scrub, chaparral, oak woodland | 3–8 ft | 3–6 ft |
| *R. ilicifolia* (hollyleaf redberry) | Foothills, chaparral, woodland | 5–10 ft | 4–8 ft |

[a]*R. californica* Cultivars: 'Eve Case' is a fast-growing selection, four to eight feet tall and wide. It is commonly grown, tolerates sun or partial shade, and prefers well-drained soil. 'Leatherleaf', featuring dark green foliage, grows to five feet with an equal spread. 'Mound San Bruno' is an adaptable shrub, tolerant of water or drought. It grows to five feet tall with a mounding habit. 'Seaview' is also adaptable and makes a dense groundcover, two feet tall and spreading four to six feet.

*Rhamnus californica*, coffeeberry

| Flowers | Culture | Comments |
| --- | --- | --- |
| Tiny umbels, May–July | Sun, dry, adaptable | Black fruits |
| Inconspicuous | Adaptable, partial shade inland | Small, spiny leaves, stiff branches, red berries |
| Small | Heat, drought-tolerant | Spiny-toothed leaves, good screen |

## *Rhododendron occidentale* — Western azalea

Ericaceae (Heath Family)

**Distribution:** Moist places and along streams in the Coast Ranges and Sierra Nevada below 7,500 ft. **Height:** 3–10 ft. **Spread:** 3–10 ft. **Exposure:** Sun to partial shade. **Water:** Regular. **Soil:** Adaptable.

The showy, fragrant flowers of western azalea make it a desirable plant for the woodland garden. Light green leaves appear in early spring, followed by glorious displays of fragrant, white or pink flowers. Western azalea is best with other shade-loving plants, such as ferns, wild ginger, salal, and barberries. It also makes an attractive container specimen for a shady location.

*Rhododendron occidentale*, Western azalea

## *RHUS* SPECIES (SUMACS)

Anacardiaceae (Sumac Family)

Three species of *Rhus* are native to California. Lemonade berry (*R. integrifolia*) and sugar bush (*R. ovata)* are closely related evergreen shrubs with handsome foliage and a profusion of flowers from mid to late spring. They are important elements of the southern California foothills and are considered to be fire-resistant. Squaw bush (*R. trilobata)* is a nontoxic, deciduous shrub that resembles poison oak (*Toxicodendron diversilobum*), which causes a severe allergic reaction in most people, but affords food and shelter to birds and small animals.

### *Rhus integrifolia* — Lemonade berry

**Distribution:** Coastal sage scrub and chaparral from Santa Barbara County to Baja California and the Channel Islands. **Height:** 3–10 ft. **Spread:** 3–10 ft. **Exposure:** Sun. **Water:** Drought-tolerant to occasional. **Soil:** Adaptable.

This dependable, evergreen shrub has a rounded form with bright green, leathery leaves and dense clusters of white or pink flowers with a long season of bloom from mid-winter into spring or summer. Small reddish fruits have an acid taste and can be made into a refreshing drink. Lemonade berry is amenable to pruning and has many landscape uses, including clipped hedges, screens, and erosion control. It can also be espaliered on a sunny wall or pruned as a groundcover for coastal gardens, where it will tolerate salt air and wind. This species grows best near the coast.

### *Rhus ovata* — Sugar bush

**Distribution:** Dry slopes, mostly in chaparral, in southern California. **Height:** 4–10 ft. **Spread:** 4–10 ft. **Exposure:** Sun. **Water:** Drought-tolerant to occasional. **Soil:** Adaptable.

Similar to lemonade bush, sugar bush has an upright or spreading habit. Dark green leaves with smooth margins are folded along the mid rib, and reddish fruits have a sugary coating. Both species are long-lived and may be combined with ceanothus, coffeeberry, and other plants with similar garden requirements. Sugar bush is adapted to hotter and drier inland areas away from the coast.

*Rhus ovata*, sugar bush

Sugar bush, clipped hedge

### ***Rhus trilobata*** **Squaw bush**

This is a deciduous, rhizomatous shrub with three-part leaves, yellow flower clusters, sticky reddish fruits, and colorful fall foliage. The berries were eaten by the California Indians, and they used the pliable stems for basketry. This shrub is common in coastal sage scrub, foothill woodland, and chaparral throughout southern California. It is useful for informal hedges.

## *RIBES* SPECIES (CURRANTS, GOOSEBERRIES)

Grossulariaceae (Gooseberry Family)

Most members of this genus are deciduous shrubs with a spreading to upright habit. Those with spines are called gooseberries, and those without are known as currants. Currants produce a profusion of flowers, usually in pendant racemes, in shades of pink, crimson, yellow, or white. Gooseberry flowers are held singly, mostly from under the slender, arching branches. Leaves are rounded, usually lobed or scalloped with serrate margins, in pale to dark shades of green. The edible fruits are enjoyed by people and wildlife, and the flowers are a source of nectar for hummingbirds.

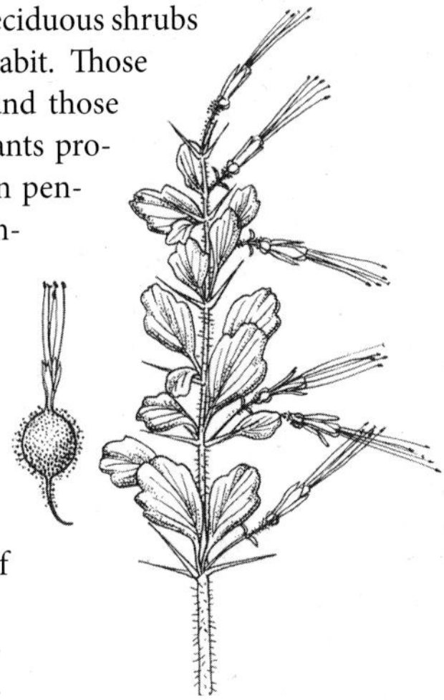

*Ribes speciosum*, fuchsia-flowered currant

In their natural habitat, the various species of *Ribes* grow among boulders or on slopes; some are indigenous to dry places and others grow in woodlands or along streams. Delicate spring flowers and clusters of berries in summer and fall give these shrubs a long season of interest. Deciduous species that go dormant in midsummer can be combined with evergreen shrubs to good advantage. Catalina perfume (*R. viburnifolium*), the evergreen currant, tolerates dry shade and is attractive year-round. It has dark green, aromatic foliage and a sprawling habit with arching branches that root where they touch the ground. Gooseberries are useful as hedges or barrier plants with their spiny stems.

**TABLE 6.** *Ribes* (Currants, Gooseberries)

| Plant | Distribution | Height | Spread |
|---|---|---|---|
| *R. aureum* (golden currant), plate | Moist places, woodland in Coast Ranges | 3–6 ft | 3–6 ft |
| *R. indecorum* (white-flowered currant) | Canyons, chaparral, So. Cal. | 6–9 ft | 4–6 ft |
| *R. malvaceum* (chaparral currant)[a] | Dry hills in Coast Ranges | 5 ft | 5 ft |
| *R. sanguineum* var. *glutinosum* (pink-flowering currant),[b] plate | Foothills and mountains | 5–12 ft | 5–12 ft |
| *R. speciosum* (fuchsia-flowered currant), figure | Chapparal and woodland, central and So. Cal. | 3–6 ft | 3–6 ft |
| *R. viburnifolium* (Catalina perfume), plate | Canyons, Santa Catalina Id. to Baja Cal. | 3 ft | 6 ft |

[a] *R. malvaceum* Cultivar: 'Montara Rose' is a coastal selection with dark pink flowers.

[b] *R. sanguineum* Cultivars: 'Spring Showers' has a neat appearance and long, pink flower clusters. 'Claremont', a Rancho Santa Ana Botanic Garden selection, has long racemes of pink flowers. 'Heart's Delight', from Marin County, is a selection with deep rose-pink flowers. 'Inverness White' has pure white flowers, and 'White Icicle' is a choice selection with white flowers on long racemes.

*Ribes sanguineum* var. *glutinosum*, pink-flowering currant

*Ribes aureum*, golden currant

| Flowers | Culture | Comments |
|---|---|---|
| Small, yellow, April to May | Sun, tolerates water | Summer berries orange to red |
| White, dense clusters, winter display | Sun to partial shade, water-tolerant | Fragrant foliage |
| Pink, drooping racemes, Oct. to March | Sun, drought-tolerant to moderate water | Purple-black berry, rough leaves lobed |
| Pink clusters, Jan. to March | Sun to partial shade, moderate water | Cultivars with pink and white flowers |
| Bright crimson, Jan. to May | Sun or shade, occasional water | Dark green leaves, prickly stems |
| Small, rose, Feb. to April | Shade, drought-tolerant | Fragrant, arching branches, evergreen |

*Ribes viburnifolium*, Catalina perfume

***Rosa californica*** **California wild rose**

Rosaceae (Rose Family)

**Distribution:** Statewide in riparian woodland below 6,000 ft. **Height:** 3–6 ft. **Spread:** 5 ft. **Exposure:** Sun to shade. **Water:** Drought-tolerant to moderate. **Soil:** Adaptable.

California wild rose is an undemanding, spring-blooming plant with fragrant, single, pink flowers. In autumn the flowers develop into orange-red fruits called rose hips. This plant has spiny stems; pinnately compound, deciduous leaves; and multiple canes that spread to form thickets. It tolerates full sun near the coast and shade inland. California wild rose provides food and shelter for birds, and it makes a good informal hedge or barrier. Deer will eat the flowers but generally ignore the foliage.

*Rosa californica*, California wild rose

***Rosa gymnocarpa*** **Wood rose**

Wood rose thrives in the shade of mixed-evergreen and coniferous forests. Plants have solitary pink flowers in the spring and grow to a height of three to five feet.

**_Simmondsia chinensis_** **Jojoba**

Simmondsiaceae (Jojoba Family)

**Distribution:** Dry slopes and canyons in southern California below 5,000 ft. **Height:** 4–10 ft. **Spread:** 6–12 ft. **Exposure:** Sun. **Water:** Drought-tolerant to occasional. **Soil:** Well-drained preferred.

Jojoba is a reliable, slow-growing shrub for hot, dry gardens. It has a rounded form and distinctive, gray-green, manzanita-like leaves. Small, greenish flowers are inconspicuous. Jojoba can be used as a clipped hedge or as a background plant. Male and female plants are required to develop the acorn-like nut, which is used to produce a high-quality oil for cosmetics and for food. In the past some wild stands were harvested, but now plantations have been established in California and Arizona as well as in other countries with a similar climate.

*Simmondsia chinensis*, jojoba

### ***Styrax officinalis redivivus*** **Snowdrop bush**

Styracaceae (Styrax Family)

**Distribution:** Chaparral and woodland in foothills of the Coast Ranges and Sierra Nevada below 3,000 ft. **Height:** 6–8 ft. **Spread:** 6 ft. **Exposure:** Sun or partial shade. **Water:** Drought-tolerant to occasional .

Snowdrop bush is a graceful, deciduous shrub with smooth, silver-gray bark. It is especially delightful when fragrant, white, bell-shaped flowers appear along the stems in May and June. This adaptable and long-lived shrub makes a fine under-planting for oaks or among shrubs and perennials with similar requirements.

### ***Styrax officinalis* var. *fulvescens*** **Southern California snowdrop bush**

This variety is native to slopes and canyons from San Luis Obispo to San Diego counties, and it varies from the species in having a tawny pubescence on the undersides of the leaves. Southern California snowdrop bush is reported to be long-lived when established, and it is outstanding when grown with low-growing ceanothus.

## *SYMPHORICARPOS* SPECIES (SNOWBERRIES)

Caprifoliaceae (Honeysuckle Family)

Snowberries are deciduous shrubs with spreading roots. Blue-green leaves are rounded and slightly lobed, and clusters of small white or pink flowers are hardly noticed. Decorative white berries persist on bare stems for a lovely winter effect. Snowberries are easy to grow, tolerant of dry shade, and useful for erosion control. They spread to form informal colonies that provide cover for wildlife.

**Distribution:** Chaparral and woodland in Coast Ranges and Sierra Nevada below 3,000 ft. **Height:** Varies by species. **Spread:** 3–6 ft. **Exposure:** Sun to shade. **Water:** Drought-tolerant to occasional. **Soil:** Adaptable.

### *Symphoricarpos albus* — Snowberry

Snowberry is an upright shrub, three to five feet tall with an equal or greater spread and tolerant of poor soil, shade, and neglect. It is most effective planted with evergreen shrubs, and it thrives in dry shade under oaks and bays.

**CULTIVARS** 'Tilden Park' is a fine selection with showy, white berries from the Regional Parks Botanic Garden. 'San Bruno Mountain' is a low form with small, white fruits. It grows up to eighteen inches tall with a spread of three to six feet.

*Symphoricarpos albus*, snowberry

***Symphoricarpos mollis*** **Creeping snowberry**

This species has arching stems less than two feet high. It combines well with plants that tolerate dry shade, such as wood fern, hummingbird sage, and woodland strawberry. Creeping snowberry spreads by rhizomes and layering stems and is useful as a groundcover on shaded slopes or under oaks.

## Trichostema lanatum — Woolly blue curls

Lamiaceae (Mint Family)

**Distribution:** Dry slopes and chaparral of Coast Ranges from Monterey and San Benito to San Diego counties. **Height:** 3–4 ft. **Spread:** 3–4 ft. **Exposure:** Sun. **Water:** Drought-tolerant to occasional. **Soil:** Well-drained.

Woolly blue curls is outstanding for its long flowering season and brilliant flower color against woolly stems covered with pink, blue, or whitish hairs. Narrow, dark green leaves have a pungent, minty aroma that is especially noticeable on warm days, and bright blue flowers are favored by hummingbirds. A number of drought-tolerant perennials and shrubs make suitable companions, including St. Catherine's lace (*Eriogonum giganteum*), fremontia (*Fremontodendron* species), and summer holly (*Comarostaphylis diversifolia*). Plants are typically short-lived and need to be replaced every few years, especially if overwatered or planted in heavy soils. Woolly blue curls can be grown in a large container as an alternative to planting it in clay soil. Its average life span is four to eight years, and it requires little attention other than an annual shearing of spent flowers.

*Trichostema lanatum*, woolly blue curls

**Vaccinium ovatum** — **Huckleberry**

Ericaceae (Heath Family)

**Distribution:** Slopes, canyons, and forests in coastal regions from Del Norte to Santa Barbara counties. **Height:** 3–8 ft. **Spread:** 3–8 ft. **Exposure:** Sun or shade. **Water:** Moderate to regular. **Soil:** Prefers acid soil.

Huckleberry is a refined and elegant garden plant with lustrous, dark green foliage. Clusters of waxy, white or pink urn-shaped flowers bloom in April and May. The fruits have long been used for pies and preserves. Except for its slow growth rate and need for acid soil, huckleberry would probably be more widely cultivated. Huckleberry is long-lived and performs well under redwoods with wild ginger and ferns. It also makes a lovely container specimen to grace an entry or shady courtyard.

*Vaccinium ovatum*, huckleberry

# PERENNIALS

California's native perennials have a wide range of ornamental qualities, and I have boundless enthusiasm and admiration for them. Perennials are herbaceous plants that live for more than two years and reach their mature size more quickly than woody plants. The plants described in this chapter are either evergreen, with a period of dormancy during part of the year, or deciduous with a persistent root system, losing their leaves during the dry season or in winter.

In the wild, various species of perennials form resplendent seaside gardens or carpet inland valleys. Some fill moist meadows and stream banks in gardenlike array. Others are the understory plants of woodlands, and many from the redwood forests have handsome foliage and delicate flowers. Most important to California gardens are the tough, sun-loving, and water-saving perennials from chaparral and arid foothills. Each in its own way can contribute a distinctive aspect to gardens.

California also has a magnificent array of ferns that grow in a variety of habitats. Several form the conspicuous understory in redwood forests, and others grow along stream banks or in rock crevices. Some species are large and bold, such as the giant chain fern (*Woodwardia fimbriata*), in contrast to the delicate five-finger fern (*Adiantum pedatum*). These and other ferns are becoming increasingly popular as garden plants.

Perennials have been used in gardens for many years, either because of their adaptability or for some element of refinement. Refined traits include attractive appearance through most of the year; foliage of good substance, color, and texture; and flowers with excellent color or abundance. Some perennials also have a delightful fragrance, unusual seeds, or value for wildlife.

Native plant enthusiasts have urged that perennials be more widely used, and drought-tolerant species have become more popular in recent years. There is a renewed interest in native irises, sages, buckwheats, penstemons, and ornamental grasses (see Grasses chapter). Properly selected, perennials can be used in many garden situations and in creative combinations. In making a selection, consideration should be given to water requirements, preference for sun or shade, rate of growth, and seasonal interest.

---

### ***Achillea millefolium*** — **Yarrow**

Asteraceae (Sunflower Family)

**Distribution:** Many plant communities throughout California. **Height:** 1–2 ft. **Spread:** 2–3 ft. **Exposure:** Sun. **Water:** Drought-tolerant to occasional. **Soil:** Adaptable.

Yarrow is a vigorous, spreading plant with finely dissected, aromatic foliage that provides winter forage for birds. Flat clusters of showy, white or pink flowers appear in late spring to early summer, attracting butterflies and bees. Cutting back old flower stems will extend the flowering season and improve appearance. Yarrow is useful for mixed borders or meadows, and it can be used as a lawn substitute because it tolerates light foot traffic and mowing. Older plants can be divided in fall or winter.

**CULTIVARS** 'Ann Gillette' has light pink flowers and gray-green leaves, and 'Island Pink' is a vigorous selection from Santa Cruz Island with pink flowers and dark green foliage. 'Calistoga' features creamy white flowers and silver-gray leaves.

*Achillea millefolium*, yarrow

---

**_Adiantum pedatum_** **Five-finger fern or maidenhair fern**
Pteridaceae (Fern Family)

**Distribution:** Moist habitats, canyon walls, and rock crevices in redwood forests, mixed evergreen forests, and chaparral from sea level to higher elevations. **Height:** 1–2 ft. tall. **Spread:** 1–2 ft. **Exposure:** Partial shade to shade. **Water:** Moderate to regular. **Soil:** Adaptable.

Five-finger fern has several fingerlike fronds with delicate finely divided foliage. Established specimens are likely to be long-lived, and old fronds can be removed to improve their appearance. They are lovely in a woodland garden with coral bells, fringe cups, and irises. The polished black stems were used by Native Americans to create decorative patterns in basketry.

*Adiantum pedatum*, five-finger fern or maidenhair fern

### *Aquilegia formosa* — Western columbine

Ranunculaceae (Buttercup Family)

**Distribution:** Moist woods and streams in northern California. **Height:** 2–3 ft. **Spread:** 1–2 ft. **Exposure:** Sun to partial shade. **Water:** Regular. **Soil:** Adaptable.

Western columbine is one of the most adaptable and dependable native perennials for a partially shaded garden. Nodding red and yellow flowers with several red spurs are carried on erect stems above light green, divided leaves. Plants bloom from May to late summer, and hummingbirds are constant visitors. Plants usually need to be replaced after two or three years.

*Aquilegia formosa*, Western columbine

### *Arabis blepharophylla* **Rose rock cress**

Brassicaceae (Mustard Family)

**Distribution:** Rocky places of coastal scrub, Santa Cruz to Sonoma counties. **Height:** 1–12 in. **Spread:** 2–12 in. **Exposure:** Sun to partial shade. **Water:** Regular. **Soil:** Well-drained.

Rose rock cress is an elegant plant with bright color and endearing charms. It has tightly clustered rosettes of deep green leaves and typical mustard flowers in vibrant pink to rose-purple from February to April. In the garden it should have morning sun with high shade in the afternoon and ample water throughout the year. Rose rock cress is not cold tolerant. It remains neat through the seasons and can be used in rock gardens and in containers.

**CULTIVAR** 'Spring Charm' is a selected strain from the Point Reyes area that produces reddish-purple flowers, mostly in spring and repeatedly in coastal areas.

### *Armeria maritima* **Sea thrift**

Plumbaginaceae (Leadwort Family)

**Distribution:** Sand dunes and coastal bluffs of central and northern California. **Height:** 6–12 in. **Spread:** 6–12 in. **Exposure:** Sun. **Water:** Occasional to moderate. **Soil:** Adaptable, well-drained preferred.

Sea thrift forms a tufted mound of evergreen, grasslike leaves. Small, round pink flowers are held on slender stalks above the foliage. They bloom from late spring to early summer, and cutting back old flowers will prolong the season of bloom. Plants tolerate full sun along the coast and prefer some shade inland. This hardy perennial is effective in front of a mixed border, along paths, and in containers.

**CULTIVAR** 'Alba' is a lovely selection with white flowers.

*Armeria maritima*, sea thrift

---

### ***Asarum caudatum*** — **Wild ginger**

Plumbaginaceae (Pipevine Family)

**Distribution:** Moist places in forests from Santa Cruz County north. **Height:** 6 in. **Spread:** 2 ft. **Exposure:** Shade. **Water:** Occasional to regular. **Soil:** Adaptable.

Wild ginger is a trailing, evergreen plant that inhabits shady, often moist, forested areas. A common groundcover in redwood forests, wild ginger is used essentially as a foliage plant because its maroon flowers are hidden among dark green, aromatic, cordate leaves. Plants are easily increased by taking rooted sections, which are freely produced on vigorous plants. This perennial can hardly be excelled as a groundcover for deep shade. Tolerant of water, wild ginger will also grow in semi-dry conditions where its growth rate will be slower. It enjoys a covering of leaf mold in autumn.

*Asarum caudatum*, wild ginger

## *ASCLEPIAS* SPECIES (MILKWEEDS)

Asclepidaceae (Milkweed Family)

Milkweeds are winter-dormant perennials with large clusters of fragrant flowers, milky sap, and wandering roots. Important nectar and larval plants for monarch butterflies, these plants perform well in dry gardens with room to spread. Coyote mint and Sonoma sage are good companions.

**Distribution:** Open slopes in North Coast Ranges and Sierra Nevada below 6,000 ft. **Height:** 2–4 ft. **Spread:** 2–4 ft. **Exposure:** Sun. **Water:** Drought-tolerant to occasional. **Soil:** Adaptable.

### *Asclepias californica* — California milkweed

California milkweed has woolly, gray leaves and umbels of pink to purple flowers.

### *Asclepias fascicularis* — Narrow-leaved milkweed

This milkweed, with its elegant pink flowers and narrow green leaves, is the favored host plant of the monarch butterfly. Watching the life cycle of a monarch butterfly is a magical experience. It begins in February and March when monarch butterflies awaken from their winter hibernation, find a mate, and migrate north from southern California or Mexico to lay their eggs on milkweed plants. An egg hatches in about four days. Then the caterpillar (larvae) eats the milkweed for about two weeks until it is fully grown, attaches itself to a stem or leaf, and transforms into a beautiful, jade-green chrysalis (pupa). Metamorphosis takes place over the next ten days before the monarch butterfly emerges from the pupa, flies away, and feeds on the flowers. This generation lives for two to six weeks and dies after laying eggs for the second generation; this is repeated until the fourth generation of butterflies migrates to warmer climates to hibernate over the winter.

### *Asclepias speciosa* — Showy milkweed

Showy milkweed is a long-lived plant with large, soft, gray-green foliage and clusters of large pink flowers. Although this is a handsome and obliging plant, it increases by underground shoots and may become a nuisance in a cultivated border.

*Asclepias speciosa*, showy milkweed

### *Coreopsis gigantea* — Giant coreopsis

Asteraceae (Sunflower Family)

**Distribution:** Sand dunes and sea bluffs from San Luis Obispo to Los Angeles County. **Height:** 3–6 ft. **Spread:** 2–4 ft. **Exposure:** Sun to partial shade. **Water:** Drought-tolerant. **Soil:** Well-drained preferred.

Giant coreopsis is a short-lived, deciduous perennial with stout, succulent stems, tufts of fern-like leaves, and clusters of bright yellow daisies. Plants may bloom from January to early summer. They require sharp drainage and do not tolerate cold or frost. Giant coreopsis is an outstanding plant for seaside gardens, and the yellow flowers are superb with purple sages.

*Coreopsis gigantea*, giant coreopsis

---

**_Dicentra formosa_** **Western bleeding heart**

Papaveraceae (Poppy Family)

**Distribution:** Woodlands and coniferous forests up to 7,000 ft in the northern Coast Ranges and Sierra Nevada. **Height:** 1.5 ft. **Spread:** 3 ft. **Exposure:** Partial to full shade. **Water:** Occasional to moderate. **Soil:** Adaptable.

This delicate, spring-blooming perennial has heart-shaped, pink or white flowers and lacy foliage. The leaves disappear when the soil dries out, returning with the winter rains. *Dicentra* means "twice spurred," from the two spurs on the heart's point. In a shaded and watered garden, western bleeding heart will increase rapidly but is easily controlled. It has few equals as a ground cover under trees and in deep shade, and the fern-like foliage affords a pleasing contrast to almost any combination of shade-loving plants. Deer sometimes rest on a bed of western bleeding heart that has naturalized under a grove of vine maples in my Lafayette garden.

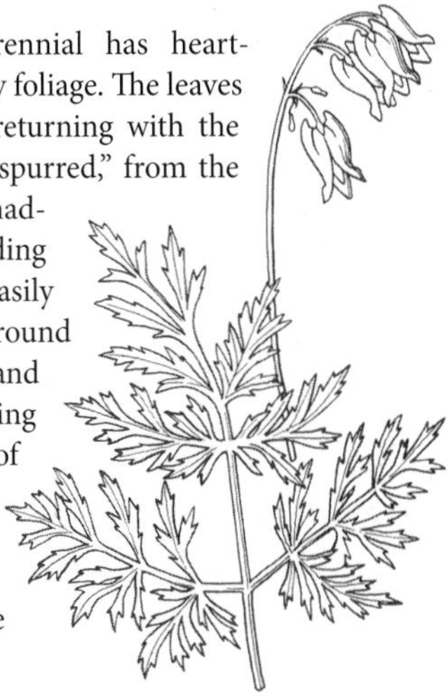

*Dicentra formosa*, Western bleeding heart

***Dodecatheon hendersonii*** **Henderson's shooting star**
Primulaceae (Primrose Family)

**Distribution:** Shaded woods and slopes in many plant communities, Coast Ranges and Sierra, Tulare County north, and in the San Bernadino Mountains. **Height:** 5–16 in. **Spread:** 4–6 in. **Exposure:** Partial shade. **Water:** Moderate. **Soil:** Well-drained.

Henderson's shooting star is known for its graceful bearing and spring flowers of reflexed corolla segments. Flower color varies from rose-pink to lilac, and occasionally white. Foliage is bright green and forms a whorl at ground level. Plants prefer some shade, especially from the afternoon sun, and, where the soil is porous, they flourish and increase abundantly. Rock gardeners have made the greatest contribution to the culture of these woodlanders. A choice combination, typical of California's foothills, is their use under redbud, since their blooming period coincides and flower color is similar. They also do well in containers or along paths where their delicate flowers can be admired at close range.

## DUDLEYA SPECIES (DUDLEYAS OR LIVE-FOREVERS)

Crassulaceae (Stonecrop Family)

*Dudleya pulverulenta*, chalk dudleya

*Dudleyas* are spectacular, long-lived succulents with silver-gray leaves that thrive in rock walls and in containers with little care. They may also be used on slopes, terraces, raised borders, or as edgings with other plants of similar requirements. Overhead water can be damaging, so it is best to plant dudleyas on an angle to allow water to drain easily. A layer of fine-textured gravel makes an effective mulch for these attractive succulents. *Dudleya pulverulenta,* chalk dudleya, is a southern California native with red flowers and large rosettes of fleshy leaves that are covered with a whitish powder. Britton dudleya, *Dudleya brittonii,* is a prized species from Baja California with similar foliage and yellow flowers.

**Distribution:** Rocky cliffs and canyons in coastal sage scrub and chaparral near the coast from San Luis Obispo County to Baja California. **Height:** 6–12 in. **Spread:** 6–12 in. **Exposure:** Sun to partial shade. **Water:** Drought-tolerant to occasional. **Soil:** Well-drained.

## *Encelia californica* — California sunflower or coast sunflower

Asteraceae (Sunflower Family)

**Distribution:** Common in coastal sage scrub and chaparral in southern California. **Height:** 3–5 ft. **Spread:** 3–5 ft. **Exposure:** Sun. **Water:** Drought-tolerant to moderate. **Soil:** Adaptable.

California sunflower blooms in spring and again in autumn. This fast-growing sub-shrub is best near the coast, although it is also found in the hills of inland valleys. The two-inch yellow sunflowers have chocolate brown centers, and spent flowers should be removed to improve its appearance. Supplemental irrigation produces more flowers and vigorous foliage. Plants should be cut back by a third in winter to promote new growth. California sunflower attracts bees, butterflies, and other insects. Ceanothus, buckwheats, and sages are natural companions for California sunflower, and it is excellent on slopes for erosion control.

---

***Epilobium canum***
***(Zauschneria californica)***
Onagraceae (Evening Primrose Family)

**California fuchsia or hummingbird fuchsia**

**Distribution:** Sunny slopes and rocky places in many plant communities. **Height:** 6 in.–4 ft. **Spread:** 3–4 ft. **Exposure:** Sun to partial shade. **Water:** Drought-tolerant to occasional. **Soil:** Adaptable, well-drained preferred.

California fuchsia makes a spectacular show from mid-summer to late fall when few other natives are blooming. Trumpet-shaped flowers, typically red-orange and occasionally pink or white, evolved to attract hummingbirds. Leaves vary in size, shape, and color from pale to medium green or a soft gray-green. The foliage often dies back in winter, and plants should be cut to the ground after flowering to prepare for new growth. Propagation by division is easily accomplished in late fall. California fuchsia is ideal for an informal garden with shrubs and grasses. It performs best in arid places with lean soil to curb its invasive tendencies. Although bota-

*Epilobium canum*, California fuchsia or hummingbird fuchsia

*Epilobium canum* 'Solidarity Pink', Solidarity Pink California fuchsia

nists have classified California fuchsias as *Epilobium*, many gardeners still refer to them as *Zauschneria*.

**CULTIVARS** There are many excellent selections with low and upright forms and varying colors of flowers and foliage. 'Schieffelin's Choice', outstanding for its refined appearance, and 'Select Mattole' both form low spreading mats just a few inches tall with silver-gray foliage and orange-red flowers. 'Solidarity Pink' is a low-growing selection with pale pink flowers and light green leaves. 'Calistoga' grows to eighteen inches in height and combines well with manzanitas and salvias. It features large, gray-green leaves and small, brilliant red flowers. 'Catalina', a Mike Evans selection from Catalina Island, grows up to three feet tall, with gray green leaves, brilliant red flowers, and a long season of bloom.

**_Erigeron glaucus_** **Seaside daisy**

Asteraceae (Sunflower Family)

**Distribution:** Coastal bluffs and coastal scrub from Santa Barbara County to Oregon. **Height:** 1 ft. **Spread:** 1–2 ft. **Exposure:** Sun. **Water:** Drought-tolerant to moderate. **Soil:** Adaptable.

Seaside daisy is a reliable perennial for a sunny border or meadow. Masses of daisylike flowers in shades of pink, rose, and lavender bloom above rosettes of soft green leaves. They will bloom from spring through fall, attracting bees and butterflies, and deadheading prolongs the season of bloom. Plants perform well in clay soils, but they usually need to be replaced after several years.

**CULTIVARS** 'Wayne Roderick' is an outstanding selection with purple flowers that does well in coastal and inland gardens. *Erigeron* 'W.R.' (for Wayne Roderick) is an adaptable cultivar that tolerates more heat than its coastal parent.

*Erigeron glaucus*, seaside daisy

## *ERIOGONUM* SPECIES (BUCKWHEATS)

Polygonaceae (Buckwheat Family)

*Eriogonum* is a large and varied genus that includes many perennials, several shrubs, and a few annuals. They are found in many habitats at practically all elevations from coastal bluffs to alpine regions, and on rocky ridges, serpentine soils, and chaparral. Buckwheats form extensive colonies along the coast and into the foothills from central to southern California. These hardy and enduring evergreen plants range in size from low, mat-forming species to the four-foot tall St. Catherine's lace. They are relatively long-lived under proper conditions, and none, to my knowledge, has invasive tendencies.

Buckwheats are foremost among California's drought-tolerant plants, and their possibilities seem almost endless. They grow from a deep root system, and the leaves in most species are basal, sometimes thick and leathery, and often felted from dense hairs on the undersides. Flowers are small and arranged in various types of inflorescences, including tight flower balls, loose clusters, and open sprays, and a few may be solitary. They bloom from spring to autumn in colors ranging from creamy white to yellows

*Eriogonum crocatum*, Conejo buckwheat

**TABLE 7.** *Eriogonum* (Buckwheats)

| Plant | Distribution | Height | Spread |
|---|---|---|---|
| *E. arborescens* (Santa Cruz Island buckwheat) | Rocky soil, Channel Ids. | 3–4 ft | 4–5 ft |
| *E. crocatum* (Conejo buckwheat), plate | Scrub and chaparral, Ventura Co. | 1.5 ft | 2 ft |
| *E. fasciculatum* (flat-topped buckwheat) | So. Cal. foothills | 1–3 ft | 4 ft |
| *E. giganteum* (St. Catherine's lace) | Channel Ids. and So. Cal. | 4–8 ft | 6–10 ft |
| *E. grande* var. *rubescens* (red-flowered buckwheat), plate | Channel Ids. and So. Cal. | 1 ft | 1 ft |
| *E. latifolium* (coast buckwheat), plate | Coastal bluffs from San Luis Obispo Co. north | 1–2 ft | 1–2 ft |
| *E. umbellatum* (sulfur buckwheat) plate, figure | Dry slopes, Nor. Cal. mtns., Sierra Nevada | 1–2 ft | 1–3 ft |

*Eriogonum umbellatum*, sulfur buckwheat

and pinks, and fading to shades of brown, russet, or deep red. These earthy tones add a lovely effect to the native garden, especially in the late summer and fall. The fruit is a hard, dry, generally one-seeded achene.

Buckwheats require full sun and lean soil. Deep irrigation may be given several times during the dry season, but most resent overhead watering. These versatile natives are relatively long-lived under proper condi-

| Flowers | Culture | Comments |
|---|---|---|
| Flat clusters, pink to rose | Tolerates some water with porous soil | Spreading, gray-green leaves, pale bark, woody |
| Flat clusters, sulfur yellow | Semi-dry | Compact |
| Flat clusters, white or pink | Drought-tolerant | Green or gray leaves, woody |
| Large, flat clusters | Dry to occasional water | Gray leaves, round form, woody |
| Round heads, pink to crimson rose | Dry to occasional water | Gray-green leaves, low mounding form |
| Small spheres, white to pale pink | Dry to occasional water | Low, rounded mounds, gray foliage |
| Dense clusters, bright yellow | Occasional water, sun to partial shade | Gray-green leaves, white underneath |

tions. They can be used with sages, golden yarrow, and woolly blue curls or planted in drifts of a single species for handsome effects. Buckwheats attract native bees and butterflies and provide food and cover for birds and small animals.

*Eriogonum grande* var. *rubescens*, red-flowered buckwheat

*Eriogonum latifolium*, coast buckwheat

### *Eriophyllum confertiflorum* — Golden yarrow

Asteraceae (Sunflower Family)

**Distribution:** Many plant communities in the Coast Ranges and Sierra foothills. **Height:** 1–2 ft. **Spread:** 3 ft. **Exposure:** Sun to partial shade. **Water:** Drought-tolerant to occasional. **Soil:** Adaptable.

Golden yarrow is an adaptable, hardy, sub-shrub with finely divided gray leaves and small, bright yellow flowers held in open cymes. These showy, evergreen plants are enduring if not overwatered, and they can be cut to the ground in late autumn for renewal. Golden yarrow is valuable for summer flowers in dry borders and suitable for inland gardens.

*Eriophyllum confertiflorum*, golden yarrow

**_Eriophyllum nevinii_** **Catalina silverlace**

This is a fast-growing, silver-leaved perennial with yellow flowers. Native to coastal scrub in central and southern California, it also grows on bluffs in the Channel Islands. Growing three feet tall with an equal spread, Catalina silverlace makes an eye-catching addition to a coastal garden. This species will need to be replaced annually in areas with frost.

---

**_Erysimum concinnum_** **Point Reyes wallflower**
Brassicaceae (Mustard Family)

**Distribution:** Coastal strand in Point Reyes area. **Height:** 12 in. **Spread:** 12 in. **Exposure:** Sun to partial shade. **Water:** Moderate to occasional. **Soil:** Well-drained preferred.

Point Reyes wallflower is a mat-forming perennial, with dark green leaves. Large heads of soft yellow to creamy white flowers have a delicate fragrance typical of this genus. They begin to bloom in February and continue into mid-spring. Butterflies are frequent visitors.

## *FRAGARIA* SPECIES (STRAWBERRIES)

Rosaceae (Rose Family)

Strawberry is a fast-growing groundcover with edible fruits and glossy, dark green leaves with three toothed leaflets. Plants spread easily by stolons.

**Distribution:** Beaches and coastal bluffs; woodlands. **Height:** 4–8 in. **Spread:** 1–2 ft. **Exposure:** Coastal species in sun; woodland in shade. **Water:** Occasional to regular. **Soil:** Adaptable.

### *Fragaria chiloensis* — Beach strawberry

This species is native to coastal beaches and bluffs of California and Chile. A parent of the commercial strawberry, beach strawberry is mainly used as a groundcover. It tolerates full sun near the coast and requires some shade inland. It is useful as a turf substitute or groundcover between larger plants. Mowing or cutting plants back in spring will stimulate new growth and prevent layering.

*Fragaria chiloensis*, beach strawberry

### *Fragaria vesca* — Woodland strawberry

Woodland strawberry is effective with ferns and irises in a shaded garden or used as a groundcover under shrubs. It produces delicious, small fruits that ripen in summer.

**_Grindelia stricta_ var. _platyphylla_** **Spreading gum plant**

Asteraceae (Sunflower Family)

**Distribution:** Coastal dunes, marshes, and bluffs in coastal scrub throughout California. **Height:** 1 ft. **Spread:** 6–10 ft. **Exposure:** Sun to partial shade. **Water:** Occasional to moderate. **Soil:** Adaptable.

This low, spreading groundcover can be used to enliven coastal gardens, spill over a wall, or enhance a meadow of native grasses. The flower buds hold a white gum, which gives the plant its name. Bright yellow, daisylike flowers bloom through the summer months, covering the stiff, green foliage. Spent flowers should be removed, and old plants can be rejuvenated by cutting them back after flowering.

**_Grindelia camporum_** **Great Valley gum plant**

**_Grindelia hirsutula_** **Gum plant**

These are tough and dependable perennials with upright habits, growing one to two feet tall. Yellow flowers bloom over a long period, attracting bees and butterflies. Grooming and deadheading improves the appearance of these sometimes coarse-looking plants. Great Valley gum plant is suited to warm inland gardens.

## *HEUCHERA* SPECIES (CORAL BELLS OR ALUM ROOTS)

Saxifragaceae (Saxifrage Family)

Even without their spring flowers, coral bells are unexcelled for shaded areas because their foliage remains attractive through the seasons. They range in size from diminutive montane species, like *H. hirsutissima* from the Santa Rosa Mountains, to larger plants native to woodlands and rocky slopes.

These compact, evergreen plants have rich green leaves, variously notched, lobed, or toothed. Slender stems rise above the foliage bearing delicate clusters of tiny, bell-shaped flowers in shades of pink and white. Coral bells are lovely planted in masses, as accents in a shaded border, or in containers. There are a number of hybrids with pleasing flowers and foliage that are vigorous and require only moderate amounts of moisture. It is easy to take cuttings from the thick neck section of the plant, rooting these in sand, and planting out after an ample root system has formed.

### *Heuchera maxima* — Island alum root

**Distribution:** Woodlands, Channel Islands. **Height:** 1–2 ft. **Spread:** 2–3 ft. **Exposure:** Sun to partial shade. **Water:** Occasional to moderate. **Soil:** Adaptable.

Island alum root has larger leaves and taller flower stems than mainland species. Creamy white flowers are long-blooming, and the foliage can be cut back every few years to renew plants.

*Heuchera maxima*, island alum root

**CULTIVARS** 'Lillian's Pink' is a lovely selection with light pink flowers and small mounds of foliage. 'Santa Ana Cardinal' displays red flowers above a compact clump of foliage.

***Heuchera micrantha*** **Crevice heuchera**

**Distribution:** Rocky slopes from Central Coast north. **Height:** 1–2 ft. **Spread:** 1–2 ft. **Exposure:** Sun to partial shade. **Water:** Occasional to moderate. **Soil:** Adaptable.

This plant grows easily in the garden and performs best in central and northern California. Flowers are white or pink, and leaves are typically basal, dark green, and sparingly hairy.
**CULTIVAR** 'Martha Roderick' displays a profusion of pink flowers.

*Heuchera micrantha*, crevice heuchera

**HYBRIDS** The Canyon Quartet series ('Canyon Belle', 'Canyon Chimes', 'Canyon Duet', and 'Canyon Melody') includes outstanding selections from the Santa Barbara Botanic Garden. They tolerate full sun in coastal gardens and prefer some shade in hot, inland areas.

## *IRIS* SPECIES (IRISES)

Iridaceae (Iris Family)

Their natural refinement and lovely flowers make native irises outstanding garden subjects. They are long-lived perennials, usually evergreen, with narrow, dark green leaves. Irises require little attention, and few plants give better performance in shaded gardens. Douglas iris starts to bloom in January or February near the coast, and mountain-dwellers bloom later in the spring.

Flowers are composed of falls (sepals) and inner standards (petals), and they bloom on erect stems. Flower colors range from pale blue, lavender, and mauve to deeper shades of blue and purple, along with yellows of varying intensity, copper, cream, and white, often with contrasting veins and color zones. With its wide spectrum of colors, iris is aptly named for the Greek goddess of the rainbow. Irises cross freely in the wild, and selections have been made of superior colors and forms.

Clumps of irises grow from creeping rhizomes, becoming larger each year. The best time to divide them is during the winter growing season. Plants also grow easily from seed, and direct seeding in autumn produces good results. Old foliage can be removed, and plants can be sheared to the ground after seed-gathering to promote new growth. A borer is attacking flower stalks and rhizomes in the Bay Area, but plants usually recover and the affected foliage is easily removed.

Irises are native to coastal bluffs, meadows, and woodlands of central and northern California. In coastal gardens they thrive in full sun with little care; inland they need protection from afternoon sun and occasional summer water. Irises are effective planted in drifts or combined with other plants with similar tolerances. They also do well in dry shade under oaks. Plants are avoided by deer and gophers. Indians used a fiber from the leaf margins for making fishing nets and game snares.

**Distribution:** Various habitats, from coastal bluffs to meadows, woodlands, and forests. **Height:** 1–2 ft. **Spread:** 1–2 ft. **Exposure:** Sun to partial shade. **Water:** Drought-tolerant to occasional. **Soil:** Adaptable.

### ***Iris douglasiana*** — **Douglas iris**

Douglas iris grows in coastal meadows from Santa Barbara County to Oregon. It blooms from February to May, and flower color ranges from blue to lavender, purple, cream, and white. 'Canyon Snow' is a choice selection and has white flowers accented with yellow blotches.

*Iris douglasiana*, Douglas iris

### ***Iris innominata*** **Del Norte iris**

This iris is a small plant with narrow leaves and brilliant yellow or purple flowers. It grows from Del Norte County north into Oregon.

### **Pacific Coast hybrid**

Pacific Coast hybrid irises display showy flowers in a wide range of colors from pastels to deep purple and maroon. The best time to make a selection is in spring when they are blooming, and fall is the optimum time for planting. Irises planted in drifts of a single color can be quite elegant, but a mix of colors is also appealing.

## *LEPECHINIA* SPECIES (PITCHER SAGES)
Lamiaceae (Mint Family)

Pitcher sages are grown for their fragrant, soft, gray-green leaves and clusters of tubular, white to pink or lavender flowers that attract bees. Plants are generally short-lived in gardens, and their form is improved by cutting back the foliage when young.

**Distribution:** Chaparral in foothills and canyons. **Height:** 3 ft. **Spread:** 4 ft. **Exposure:** Sun to partial shade. **Water:** Drought-tolerant to occasional. **Soil:** Adaptable.

### ***Lepechinia calycina*** — **Pitcher sage**

Pitcher sage has white to pale pink flowers and occurs statewide.

*Lepechinia calycina*, pitcher sage

### ***Lepechinia fragrans*** — **Fragrant pitcher sage**

This species is native to southern California and blooms in spring and summer. Flowers are lavender, and the foliage has a delightful scent.

**_Lewisia cotyledon_** **Cliff-maids or broadleaf lewisia**
Portulacaceae (Purslane Family)

**Distribution:** Rock outcrops and canyon walls in the Siskiyou Mountains above 1,500 ft. **Height:** 1 ft. **Spread:** 10 in. **Exposure:** Sun to partial shade. **Water:** Drought-tolerant to occasional. **Soil:** Well-drained.

Named for Meriwether Lewis, this plant has long been popular for rock gardens and containers. It is characterized by basal rosettes of fleshy, evergreen leaves, and short panicles of showy white flowers with red veins. Plants are frost hardy and require good drainage. They prefer to be planted sideways so moisture drains away from their crowns, as they grow in rock walls. They also do well in containers with a fast-draining soil mix. Hybrids are available in a variety of flower colors.

*Lewisia cotyledon*, cliff-maids or broadleaf lewisia

**_Lupinus albifrons_** **Silver bush lupine**
Fabaceae (Pea Family)

**Distribution:** Dry slopes in many plant communities of the Coast Ranges, Transverse Ranges, and Sierra Nevada below 5,000 ft. **Height:** 5 ft. **Spread:** 5 ft. **Exposure:** Sun. **Water:** Drought-tolerant to occasional. **Soil:** Well-drained.

In spite of their presence in almost every type of terrain, lupines are seldom thought of as garden materials. They are easily recognized for their pea-shaped flowers and palmately compound leaves. Lupines vary in size and are adapted to open, sunny areas with well-drained soil. Silver bush lupine has attractive gray-green foliage and graceful spikes of blue-purple flowers. Although cultivated lupines are generally short-lived, they often produce volunteer seedlings as replacements. Lupines can be combined with Sonoma sage, coyote mint, and an assortment of native bulbs and grasses.

*Lupinus albifrons*, silver bush lupine

***Lupinus arboreus*** **Yellow bush lupine**

Yellow bush lupine grows along the coast from Sonoma to Ventura counties, but it is not recommended for gardens from Mendocino County northward because it has become an invasive weed there and a threat to local species. Despite its name, this lupine has yellow or blue flowers and green foliage. It is stunning combined with deer grass in an informal garden. Seeds may be gathered when ripe and stored until planting time or left to reseed freely on their own. It is best to remove old flower heads and tough stems for neatness and to encourage the development of a leafy base.

*Lupinus arboreus*, yellow bush lupine

## *MIMULUS* SPECIES (BUSH MONKEYFLOWERS OR STICKY MONKEYFLOWERS)

Scophulariaceae (Figwort Family)

Bush monkeyflowers have much to offer gardeners, being adaptable to cultivation under conditions similar to their natural ones. Considered by some botanists to be in the genus *Diplacus,* bush monkeyflowers occupy varied habitats in California from arid, rocky foothills to moist slopes, stream banks, and meadows. They bloom through spring and summer, with a profusion of flowers in lively colors.

All have tubular flowers with lobes and markings that give them their quaint, face-like appearance and common name. Their sticky leaves are lance-shaped and arranged in

*Mimulus guttatis*, common monkeyflower

*Mimulus* hybrids, monkeyflower hybrids

**TABLE 8.** *Mimulus* (Monkeyflowers)

| Plant | Distribution | Height | Spread |
|---|---|---|---|
| *M. aurantiacus* (sticky monkeyflower)[a] | Dry foothills | 2–3 ft | 2–3 ft |
| *M. bifidus* (azalea-flowered monkeyflower) | Rocky foothills | 1–2 ft | 2–3 ft |
| *M. cardinalis* (scarlet monkeyflower) | Streams and moist places | 1–2 ft | 1–2 ft |
| *M. guttatus* (common monkeyflower), plate | Common in wet places | 1–3 ft | 1–3 ft |
| *M. hybrids* (monkeyflower hybrids), plate | Cultivars | 1–3 ft | 1–3 ft |

[a]*M. aurantiacus* Cultivar: 'Dark Gulch' is a selection from Mendocino County with larger peach-colored flowers and purple highlights.

pairs along the stems. Flowers, especially the hybrid selections, display an amazing range of colors in shades of orange, red, pink, purple, yellow, white, and cream.

Bush monkeyflowers are short-lived perennials, easily replaced by tip cuttings of young plants. In inland gardens they prefer some shade, and near the coast they tolerate full sun. Occasional summer water improves their appearance in inland regions, and light pruning is helpful to shape plants and stimulate a second bloom in late summer or fall. These showy perennials are colorful additions to a native garden, and they combine well with California sagebrush and grasses. They also attract hummingbirds.

**CULTIVARS** The following selections represent a few of the best introductions, and enthusiasts will find many more to choose from. 'Burgundy' has deep red flowers, 'Eleanor' is a notable selection with pale yellow flowers, and 'Verity White' features creamy white flowers.

| Flowers | Culture | Comments |
|---|---|---|
| Soft orange | Sun to partial shade | Long-lived |
| Buff to apricot | Partial shade inland | Attractive flowers, glossy leaves |
| Red | Sun or shade, ample water | Long bloom |
| Yellow with brown spots | Adaptable, sun or light shade, water | Spreads by stolons, often weedy |
| Many | Sun or partial shade, good drainage | Short-lived, showy |

## *MONARDELLA* SPECIES (COYOTE MINTS)

Lamiaceae (Mint Family)

These free-flowering perennials are long-lived under semi-dry conditions. They have aromatic leaves and stems that rise above the foliage bearing tubular flowers in dense heads, surrounded by bracts. Coyote mints are excellent with buckwheats, penstemons, and other drought-tolerant plants.

### *Monardella macrantha* — Scarlet coyote mint

**Distribution:** Chaparral and woodlands from the Santa Lucia Mountains to San Diego County. **Height:** 6 in. **Spread:** Spreading. **Exposure:** Sun. **Water:** Occasional to moderate. **Soil:** Well-drained preferred.

Clusters of red-orange flowers are visited by hummingbirds through the summer months. Once established, scarlet coyote mint spreads to form mats of dark green foliage. It is useful in dry borders and on slopes where the colorful flowers can show to advantage. 'Marian Sampson' is a fine selection that requires little care.

## *Monardella villosa* — **Coyote mint**

**Distribution:** Rocky slopes from Humboldt to San Luis Obispo counties. **Height:** 1–2 ft. **Spread:** 1–2 ft. **Exposure:** Sun. **Water:** Drought-tolerant to moderate. **Soil:** Well-drained.

Coyote mint is one of California's most useful and accommodating perennials for dry slopes, rock gardens, or containers. It has gray-green leaves and lavender to rose-purple flowers that attract butterflies. Removing spent flowers improves their appearance and prolongs their season of bloom. Cutting plants back in fall or winter promotes denser growth for the following year. Native Americans made a tea from the leaves.

*Monardella villosa*, coyote mint

***Oxalis oregana*** **Redwood sorrel**

Oxalidaceae (Wood Sorrel Family)

**Distribution:** Coastal forests from Monterey County to the Northwest. **Height:** 4–8 in. **Spread:** Spreading. **Exposure:** Shade. **Water:** Occasional to moderate. **Soil:** Adaptable.

This low groundcover is common in redwood forests, where it grows in deep shade with western sword fern, wild ginger, and inside-out flower. Clover-like leaves are trifoliate, and the leaflets fold in sun or drought. Small flowers are white to purple on single stalks just above the foliage. Once established, this plant spreads rapidly by rhizomes and is easily controlled, unlike the weedy Bermuda buttercup (*O. pes-caprae*) that is native to South Africa.

*Oxalis oregana*, redwood sorrel

## *PENSTEMON* SPECIES (PENSTEMONS)

Scrophulariaceae (Figwort Family)

*Penstemon* is a superb genus with over fifty species native to California. They grow in many habitats, including rocky inclines, dry slopes, woodlands, and meadows at many elevations. Brilliant flower color is an outstanding feature of penstemons in shades of blue, purple, pink, red, and occasionally white or yellow. Flowers are tubular with the lower lips cleft into lobes. They are frequently visited by hummingbirds. Foliage is evergreen and well-disposed along the stems, giving plants a neat appearance through the seasons.

Most penstemons are self-contained, free-flowering, and adaptable to garden culture. As a rule they prefer sun and lean, porous, well-drained soil, and they may be watered during their period of active growth. Cutting back spent flowers encourages a repeat bloom. Their longevity depends on growing conditions, and rich soil along with overwatering tends to shorten their life span. The ease of producing new plants from cuttings makes their replacement simple. Cuttings should be taken from young, basal shoots rather than from old, woody portions. New cultivars with rich flower colors are being introduced, and the selection can change from year to year.

*Penstemon azureus*, azure penstemon

**TABLE 9.** *Penstemon* (Penstemons)

| Plant | Distribution | Height | Spread |
|---|---|---|---|
| *P. azureus* (azure penstemon), figure | Dry slopes, northern mountains | 1–2 ft | 2–3 ft |
| *P. centranthifolius* (scarlet buglar) | Chaparral, foothills, and canyons | 1–2 ft | 1 ft |
| *P. heterophyllus* (foothill penstemon),[a] plate | Grasslands, chaparral, and woodlands | 1–2 ft | 2 ft |
| *P. spectabilis* (royal penstemon) | Coastal sage scrub, chaparral | 2–3 ft | 3 ft |

[a] *P. heterophyllus* Cultivars: 'Blue Springs' has narrow, green leaves and bright blue flower spikes. 'Margarita BOP' (Bottom of the Porch), a fine introduction from Las Pilitas Nursery, features blue-purple flowers in spring and early summer.

*Penstemon heterophyllus*, foothill penstemon

| Flowers | Culture | Comments |
|---|---|---|
| Blue, May to Aug. | Sun, semi-dry | Vigorous, spreading |
| Narrow tubular, red, April to July | Sun, moderate water to dry | Glaucus gray-green leaves |
| Blue or rose-violet | Water-tolerant, free flowering | Good in rock gardens, mixed borders |
| Tall spikes, lavender-purple | Sun, well-drained | Short-lived |

***Polystichum munitum*** **Western sword fern**

Dryopteridaceae (Wood Fern Family)

**Distribution:** Coastal forests and woodlands from Monterey to Del Norte counties. **Height:** 2–3 ft. **Spread:** 2–3 ft. **Exposure:** Partial shade to shade. **Water:** Occasional to regular. **Soil:** Adaptable.

*Polystichum munitum*, Western sword fern

Western sword fern is probably the most adaptable native fern, thriving in humus-rich soil and requiring little moisture when established. Dark green, pinnate blades with sword-shaped leaflets are upright and spreading. This fern is excellent in dry shade under oaks, with coral bells and irises or planted with western bleeding heart and wild ginger under redwoods. It grows in deep shade and tolerates half-day sun near the coast or filtered shade inland. Plants may be increased by division of the rhizome in early spring, keeping it moist and shaded until new growth begins.

***Ranunculus californicus*** **California buttercup**

Ranunculaceae (Buttercup Family)

**Distribution:** Foothill grasslands and open woodlands near the coast and inland. **Height:** 1–2 ft. **Spread:** 1 ft. **Exposure:** Sun to partial shade. **Water:** Drought-tolerant to occasional. **Soil:** Adaptable.

California buttercup brightens meadows in early spring with shiny yellow flowers that continue blooming until the soil dries out. The flowers are held on wiry stems a foot or more above the basal foliage. They re-seed freely, and the flower stalks should be cut back in the autumn after the seeds have dropped. This delicate perennial is effective with native bulbs and grasses.

*Ranunculus californicus*, California buttercup

---

**_Romneya coulteri_** **Matilija poppy**

Papaveraceae (Poppy Family)

**Distribution:** Coastal sage scrub and chaparral in Southern California. **Height:** 3–8 ft. **Spread:** 8 ft or more. **Exposure:** Sun to partial shade. **Water:** Drought-tolerant to occasional. **Soil:** Adaptable.

This statuesque poppy has long been admired and cultivated by gardeners for its spectacular flowers and handsome foliage. Large, fragrant flowers have crinkled white petals surrounding a cluster of golden yellow stamens, and gray-green leaves are deeply cut. Matilija poppy blooms in spring and summer and should be cut back to the ground after flowering. New leaves appear with the winter rains. Notoriously difficult to start, this plant is difficult to control once established. Its tendency to spread makes it too rampant for small gardens. Excellent on dry slopes for erosion control, Matilija poppy can be combined with ceanothus and fremontia in large-scale plantings.

*Romneya coulteri*, Matilija poppy

## *SALVIA* SPECIES (SAGES)

Lamiaceae (Mint Family)

*Salvia* is a large genus with hundreds of species worldwide. Most of California's native sages are perennials. All have aromatic foliage, square stems, and tubular, two-lipped flowers arranged in whorls on flower stems or clustered in spikes. Most species inhabit dry places and are easy to grow. Those described here are valued for their spectacular flowers and attractive foliage. Whorls of dried seed heads add interest after flowering, and cutting plants back in late summer or fall helps retain their attractive appearance. Plants can be propagated by cuttings or by dividing species that spread by rhizomes. Sonoma sage roots frequently along the creeping stems, and new plants are easily obtained.

Some sages are spreading and others have a mounding or upright habit. They can be used on slopes or as accents in the garden, combined with other plants with similar horticultural requirements. Sonoma sage is an ideal groundcover for hot, dry slopes in full sun. Hummingbird

*Salvia spathacea*, hummingbird sage

*Salvia apiana*, white sage

*Salvia sonomensis*, Sonoma sage

sage thrives in dry shade with room to spread, but it can be difficult to control in sunny areas once it begins to spread. The competition of other plants keeps it within bounds in wooded areas. Purple sage has a mounding form and striking silver-gray foliage, and Cleveland sage is useful for erosion control and ornamental purposes.

Sages attract butterflies and hummingbirds, and their nectar produces a delicate honey. Native Americans used the leaves of black sage, *S. mellifera*, for tea and early settlers used them for seasoning food. Cleveland sage is also recommended as a seasoning for food.

**CULTIVARS** A number of hybrid sages are popular in gardens, including 'Allen Chickering' with its mounding habit, dark green leaves, and blue-purple flowers. 'Bee's Bliss' has gray-green leaves with lavender-pink flower spikes and a low spreading form, and 'Dara's Choice' is a vigorous groundcover with green leaves and dark lavender flowers.

*Salvia clevelandii*, Cleveland sage

**TABLE 10.** *Salvia* (Sages)

| Plant | Distribution | Height | Spread |
|---|---|---|---|
| *S. apiana* (white sage), plate | 3 Coastal sage scrub, chaparral, So. Cal. | 3–5 ft | 5 ft |
| *S. clevelandii* (Cleveland sage),[a] plate | Coastal sage scrub, chaparral, So. Cal. | 3 ft | 4 ft |
| *S. leucophylla* (purple sage)[b] | Coastal sage scrub, So. Cal. | 3–4 ft | 4–6 ft |
| *S. mellifera* (black sage)[c] | Coastal sage scrub, chaparral | 3–5 ft | 4–6 ft |
| *S. sonomensis* (Sonoma sage),[d] plate | Chaparral, woodland | 8 in. | 3 ft+ |
| *S. spathacea* (hummingbird sage),[e] figure | Many plant communities | 2 ft | 3 ft+ |

[a]*S. clevelandii* Cultivar: 'Winifred Gilman' is an excellent, drought-tolerant selection with deep violet flowers and reddish flower stems. 'Allen Chickering' is a hybrid between *S. clevelandii* and *S. leucophylla*, with lavender-blue flowers.

[b]*S. leucophylla* Cultivar: 'Amethyst Bluff' has rosy-pink flowers and silver foliage, mounding to five feet. 'Figueroa' is a compact selection, spreading to four feet, with lavender-pink flowers and gray foliage.

## *Satureja douglasii* — Yerba buena

Lamiaceae (Mint Family)

**Distribution:** Chaparral and woodland. **Height:** 6 in. **Spread:** 3 ft or more. **Exposure:** Partial shade to shade. **Water:** Occasional to moderate. **Soil:** Adaptable, well-drained preferred.

This trailing mint gave San Francisco its original name, Yerba buena, meaning "good herb" in Spanish. Small, green leaves have scalloped edges, and tiny white flowers appear in spring. This fragrant groundcover is useful between stepping stones or planted in containers in a shaded area where its trailing stems can spill over and extend into the garden. Native Americans dried the leaves for an aromatic tea, and fresh leaves add a minty flavor to iced tea.

| Flowers | Culture | Comments |
|---|---|---|
| White spikes, spring | Sun, drought-tolerant | Silver foliage, aromatic |
| Purple | Sun, dry, some forms tender | Woody subshrub, upright |
| Pink-purple, spring-summer | Sun, dry | Gray-green leaves, mounding |
| Pale blue or white, spring | Sun, part shade, dry | Dark green leaves, erect habit |
| Blue-violet, spring | Sun, dry | Glaucus foliage, spreading |
| Crimson, spring | Shade, dry | Spreads by rhizomes, invasive tendencies |

[c]*S. mellifera* Cultivar: 'Tera Seca' is a fast-growing selection with pale lavender flowers, one to two feet tall, and spreading to eight feet. It is useful as a groundcover for sunny, dry slopes.

[d]*S. sonomensis* Cultivar: 'Dara's Choice' has gray-green leaves and grows well in part shade. 'Hobbit Toes' forms a compact mat with gray foliage and blue-violet flowers.

[e]*S. spathacea* Cultivar: 'Alvis Keedy' is a yellow-flowered selection from Santa Barbara County.

*Satureja douglasii*, yerba buena

**_Sedum spathulifolium_** **Sedum or stonecrop**

Crassulaceae (Stonecrop Family)

**Distribution:** Cliffs from coast to foothills. **Height:** 3–6 in. **Spread:** 3–6 in. **Exposure:** Sun to partial shade. **Water:** Occasional. **Soil:** Well-drained.

This fine-textured succulent grows on coastal bluffs and rocky walls in foothill regions. It has bright yellow starlike flowers and tight rosettes of leaves that may be green or gray, sometimes edged with red or purple. Sedum makes a good accent or filler in rock gardens and containers. 'Cape Blanco' is a choice cultivar with silver leaves.

*Sedum spathulifolium*, sedum or stonecrop

**_Sidalcea malviflora_** **Checkerbloom**

Malvaceae (Mallow Family)

**Distribution:** Coastal grasslands and meadows. **Height:** 6 in. to 2 ft. **Spread:** 2 ft. **Exposure:** Sun to partial shade. **Water:** Drought-tolerant to moderate. **Soil:** Adaptable.

This spring-blooming perennial is common in grasslands throughout California. Showy flowers resemble hollyhocks in shades of pink and rose, and dark green leaves are rounded and lobed. Plants can be spreading or upright, and they are attractive in a meadow garden with blue-eyed grass and seaside daisy. They are easy to grow in containers and have a long season of bloom when spent flowers are removed.

*Sidalcea malviflora*, checkerbloom

---

**Sisyrinchium bellum** — **Blue-eyed grass**

Iridaceae (Iris Family)

**Distribution:** Widespread in many plant communities from San Diego to Humboldt counties. **Height:** 4–12 in. **Spread:** 6–12 in. **Exposure:** Sun to partial shade. **Water:** Occasional to moderate. **Soil:** Adaptable.

Blue-eyed grass is aptly named, with its narrow, dark green, grass-like leaves and vibrant blue-purple, occasionally white, six-petaled flowers surrounding a central cone of yellow stamens. Plants re-seed generously, and clumps can be divided in late fall or early spring. Blue-eyed grass is delightful in front of a mixed border, along paths, or in containers. I have combined it with sulfur buckwheat and California fescue, and Marjorie Schmidt grew an assortment of spring-blooming annuals with blue-eyed grass.

**CULTIVAR** 'Rocky Point' is a vigorous, dwarf selection with wide blades and blue-purple flowers.

**Sisyrinchium californicum** — **Yellow-eyed grass**

Yellow-eyed grass grows in moist places from Monterey County northward. It forms a clump of grass-like leaves with yellow flowers. This species does best in a sunny, watered garden. It re-seeds freely, and the foliage is easily removed when it dies back in late summer.

*Sisyrinchium californicum*, yellow-eyed grass

---

## *Solidago californica* — California goldenrod

Asteraceae (Sunflower Family)

**Distribution:** Open areas below 7,000 ft, including meadows and woodlands. **Height:** 1–2 ft. **Spread:** 3 ft or more. **Exposure:** Sun to partial shade. **Water:** Drought-tolerant to moderate. **Soil:** Adaptable.

California goldenrod brightens gardens from late summer through fall with wands of golden yellow flowers and makes a lovely autumn accent in a meadow of native grasses. This vigorous perennial spreads by creeping rhizomes and may become invasive with irrigation. Plants are easy to control, and spent flowers should be removed.

*Solidago californica*, California goldenrod

### ***Tellima grandiflora*** — **Fringe cups**

Saxifragaceae (Saxifrage Family)

**Distribution:** Moist woods and along streams from central California northward. **Height:** 1.5–2 ft. **Spread:** 18 in. **Exposure:** Partial shade to shade. **Water:** Regular. **Soil:** Adaptable.

The lobed, basal foliage of fringe cups resembles coral bells, and the small, cupped flowers have fringed petals in shades of green, white, or pink. They bloom on tall, slender stems that rise a foot or more above the leaves. Fringe cups are lovely with ferns and wild ginger in a woodland garden.

---

### ***Vancouveria planipetala*** — **Inside-out flower**

Berberidaceae (Barberry Family)

**Distribution:** Coastal forests from Monterey County northward. **Height:** 1 ft. **Spread:** 1 ft. **Exposure:** Shade. **Water:** Occasional to moderate. **Soil:** Adaptable.

Inside-out flower has attractive, dark green, rounded leaves and a compact, creeping habit. Plants spread slowly by rhizomes and persist where winters are mild. Tiny white flowers on wiry stems have reflexed petals for an inside-out effect. This refined groundcover is superb with irises and huckleberry. Inside-out flower has naturalized under a grove of vine maples in my garden, where it thrives in shade with occasional irrigation.

#### ***Vancouveria hexandra*** — **Northern inside-out flower**

Northern inside-out flower is a delicate plant with light green leaves. It increases rapidly with ample water in shaded areas and dies back in winter.

*Vancouveria hexandra*, northern inside-out flower

### *Woodwardia fimbriata* — Giant chain fern

Blechnaceae (Deer Fern Family)

**Distribution:** Along streams and moist places throughout California. **Height:** 4–6 ft. **Spread:** 3–4 ft. **Exposure:** Partial shade to shade. **Water:** Occasional to regular. **Soil:** Adaptable.

Giant chain fern has an upright and arching form, and plants are long-lived once established. It is drought-tolerant in coastal areas and requires summer irrigation in inland gardens. Old fronds can be removed to improve its appearance. The largest of California's native ferns, it is outstanding in a woodland garden or by a shaded wall.

*Woodwardia fimbriata*, giant chain fern

# ANNUALS

Spectacular displays of annual wildflowers were once a glorious feature of the countryside. Vast flowery plains covered many areas of the state, especially around the great Central Valley, where small, free-flowering species formed floral carpets in early spring. Many wildflowers remain, but most of them are greatly reduced. Mesas, meadows, seemingly bald hills, open woodlands, and sections of the coastal plains all support their particular combinations of annuals, mostly blooming in the early spring. Sweeping masses of poppies, lupines, and other annuals can still be seen in some areas. Tidy tips enliven the open hills, and meadowfoam brightens vernal pools. Although most of these annuals require full sun, shaded oak woodlands are sometimes decorated with the elegant red ribbons of clarkia and the delicate spires of collinsia.

Some of the best places to see outstanding wildflower displays are the Antelope Valley California Poppy Reserve in Lancaster, Bear Valley in Colusa County, Carrizo Plains in San Luis Obispo County, Hunter-Liggett military reservation near Jolon in Monterey County, and Point Reyes National Seashore. The timing varies from year to year, beginning with the first blooms in mid-February near the coast. Inland valleys come to life in March and April, and the wildflower season extends from mid-April through mid-summer in the mountains.

Although carpets of wild annuals cannot be duplicated on nature's grand scale, it is possible to use them in gardens on a smaller scale to capture some of the magic of the California spring. Drifts of bird's eye gilia complement many other flower choices, Chinese houses make a delicate splash of color in filtered shade, and blazing star is a choice plant for a sunny rock garden. These and other native annuals may be used for masses of a single color, in mixtures to broadcast in open areas, in a meadow with native grasses, or for color among other natives. Growing annuals in containers is an easy way to add color to any garden.

Annual wildflowers complete their life cycle in one year or less, and they are ideally suited to California's Mediterranean climate. They germinate with the winter rains, bloom in spring, and set seeds before the soil dries out in summer. Plants then wither and die after producing a supply of seeds for the following year. Annuals grow readily from seed with the correct combination of sun and moisture, and some also require a number of cool nights or nights with frost. Planting a variety of species can provide a succession of bloom from late winter through the spring.

Autumn is the best time to broadcast seeds of annual wildflowers, ideally just before the first rains so the moisture can aid in their germination. Seeds sown in the spring will usually require irrigation until they have germinated. Some experts recommend that seed be scuffed into the soil as soon as it is ripe to simulate nature's buffeting winds and pounding rain. Areas to be planted should be raked or lightly cultivated and as free of weeds as possible. Mix the seeds with sand or soil before scattering them over the prepared soil. After sowing, rake the seeds gently to make firm contact with the soil, and add a light layer of mulch or leaf litter to prevent birds or other animals from disturbing the seeds.

An alternative to sowing seeds in the garden is to start them in flats or four-inch pots. This method also solves the problems of early predation or drying out of just-sprouted seedlings. When well-rooted, the seedlings can be thinned and transplanted to the garden with minimal root disturbance. A number of annuals are also available in nurseries in early spring and ready for planting. Most prefer lean soil and moderate amounts of water unless they are native to areas of abundant moisture. Too much water, especially with rich soil, causes leafiness and straggly growth at the expense of flowers. Late spring rains and supplemental irrigation can extend their season of bloom.

Seeds of wild annuals, which are adaptable to cultivation, are available from several specialists. Some of the most beautiful and easily grown annual wildflowers are described in this chapter.

## *CLARKIA* SPECIES (CLARKIAS)

Onagraceae (Evening Primrose Family)

Named for Captain William Clark of the 1804 Lewis and Clark Expedition, the ornamental qualities of clarkias were recognized as early as 1840 from seed sent to England by David Douglas and other explorers. Selected strains of elegant clarkia soon appeared in seed catalogs, and it continues to be a favorite annual wildflower. Horticultural selections from other species have produced the wide assortment of clarkias now available.

Clarkias have two flower shapes: those with the four petals in a cup-shaped flower (*C. amoena*, *C. purpurea*, *C. rubicunda*) formerly known as godetias, and others with a wheel- or spokelike arrangement (*C. concinna*, *C. unguiculata*). Warm flower colors are further enhanced in some species by blotches or spots of darker colors. The flowers close up at night and each lasts several days.

These adaptable, free-flowering, and beautifully marked and colored annuals bloom from late spring into summer. They may be grown from seed broadcast in autumn and again in spring to extend the season of bloom. Clarkias are effective in masses, either

*Clarkia amoena*, farewell to spring

*Clarkia purpurea*, purple clarkia

**TABLE 11.** *Clarkia* (Clarkias)

| Plant | Distribution | Height | Spread |
|---|---|---|---|
| *C. amoena* (farewell to spring), figure | Coastal bluffs, Marin to Humboldt Cos. | 1–3 ft | 1–3 ft |
| *C. concinna* (red ribbons clarkia), figure | Woodlands and forests, central and Nor. Cal. | 18 in. | 2 ft |
| *C. purpurea* (purple clarkia), plate | Dry slopes, cismontane Cal. | 18 in. | 2 ft |
| *C. rubicunda* (herald of summer) | Central Coast | 12–18 in. | 1–2 ft |
| *C. unguiculata* (elegant clarkia), plate | Widespread in grasslands, chaparral, and woodlands | 1–4 ft | 1–3 ft |

of a single color or in mixtures. Elegant clarkia is lovely with native grasses in a sunny meadow, and few plants have more luminous flowers than red ribbons clarkia, which is unmatched for shade. Native Americans enjoyed eating the dried seeds of elegant clarkia.

*Clarkia concinna*, red ribbons clarkia

| Flowers | Culture | Comments |
| --- | --- | --- |
| Cup-shaped, lavender-pink, crimson center, June–Aug. | Sun, moderate moisture | Late spring bloom, good in mixed borders |
| Circular, slashed and lobed, deep pink, May–July | High shade, moisture, leaf mold in soil | Lively color, good in containers |
| Cup-shaped, rose-purple, May–July | Sun, semi-dry | Plant with bulbs or annuals |
| Cup-shaped, rose-pink, darker base, May–Sept. | Sun, semi-dry | Long-blooming |
| Circular, lobed, pink, purple or salmon, April–June | Sun, water | Showy, robust |

*Clarkia unguiculata*, elegant clarkia

## *Claytonia perfoliata* — Miner's lettuce

Portulacaceae (Purslane Family)

**Distribution:** Widespread in moist areas from central California northward. **Height:** 6 in. **Spread:** 6 in. **Exposure:** Partial shade to shade. **Water:** Moderate to regular. **Soil:** Adaptable.

*Claytonia perfoliata*, miner's lettuce

Miner's lettuce is an edible annual that is easy to identify by its perfoliate leaf, a round disk surrounding the stem. Delicious in salads, this plant was eaten by Native Americans and early settlers. Miner's lettuce re-seeds freely in moist, shaded areas to form colonies that die back in summer and return with the rains.

## *Collinsia heterophylla* — Chinese houses

Scrophylariaceae (Figwort Family)

**Distribution:** Common in shady woods and many plant communities of cismontane California. **Height:** 1–2 ft. **Spread:** 1 ft. **Exposure:** Partial shade. **Water:** Regular. **Soil:** Adaptable.

A member of the snapdragon family, this delicate wildflower is distinctive for its pagoda-like inflorescence. Arranged in whorls on the stem, the upper lip of each flower is white to pale lilac, and the lower is violet to rose-purple. Leaves are bright green with serrate margins. Seeds sown in fall will bloom in April and May, and they will self-sow in favorable conditions. When plants are robust, they can be sheared back for a second flowering. Seeded in late spring, plants will bloom about September. Chinese houses are ideal for a shaded border or massed among trees and shrubs.

*Collinsia heterophylla*, Chinese houses

---

***Eschscholzia californica*** **California poppy**

Papaveraceae (Poppy Family)

**Distribution:** Common in fields and foothills throughout California. **Height:** 8–24 in. **Spread:** 2 ft. **Exposure:** Sun. **Water:** Occasional to moderate. **Soil:** Adaptable, well-drained preferred.

Early Spanish explorers sailing along the California coast observed the hills blazing with orange-colored poppies and described it as the "land of fire." They named the flower *copa de oro*, meaning cup of gold. The California poppy was chosen as the state flower in 1903 for its wide distribution, brilliant color, satiny flowers, and long flowering period. Depending on climate and exposure, plants may bloom from February all through the summer.

Poppies have cup-shaped petals in colors that range from pale yellow to deep orange and occasionally white. The California poppy is distinguished by having a double rim or platform that supports the bud, the flower, and later, the seed pod. Leaves are gray-green and finely dissected. Plants often become large by the end of their first season, and they grow from carrotlike taproots, which may persist for several years. Old plants that have become straggly may be cut to near the ground level in autumn.

Poppies are among the most adaptable of all wildflowers, and they require little in the way of water or cultivation. Plants often produce a second bloom if cut back after flowering. They re-seed freely and may intrude

*Eschscholzia californica*, California poppy

where they are not wanted. These colorful annuals are valuable for dry, sunny areas with other wildflowers and grasses. Selections are available with single and double flowers in an impressive range of colors, including cream, rose, crimson, flame, and shades of yellow and orange. These are useful in gardens with a special color scheme or planted with other spring wildflowers. The orange-flowered poppies will predominate over time if they are grown with the other color forms.

### *Eschscholzia caespitosa* **Tufted poppy**

This poppy is native to valley grasslands and grows to six inches with bright yellow flowers and pale, blue-green foliage. It performs well in sunny areas of the garden and in containers.

***Gilia tricolor*** **Bird's eye gilia**

Polemoniaceae (Phlox Family)

**Distribution:** Valley grasslands and slopes throughout California. **Height:** 6–12 in. **Spread:** 8 in. **Exposure:** Sun to partial shade. **Water:** Occasional to moderate. **Soil:** Adaptable.

This reliable annual blooms from April into early summer. Flowers are pale blue or violet with a yellow throat surrounded by a dark purple ring. The leaves are dissected into narrow segments. Plants are small, often slender and delicate in appearance. Gilias may be planted from seed broadcast in late autumn to early spring, but they germinate more freely when planted with the early autumn rains. They require little attention and perpetuate themselves by volunteers. Bird's eye gilia is lovely mixed with other annuals or planted in drifts of a solid color.

***Gilia capitata*** **Globe gilia**

Globe gilia grows in open areas and mixed evergreen forests in the Coast Ranges from Marin County north. It produces small, dense, terminal heads of powder blue flowers on one- to two-foot stems and has a long flowering period.

***Lasthenia californica*** **Goldfields**

Asteraceae (Sunflower Family)

**Distribution:** Moist habitats throughout California. **Height:** 4–12 in. **Spread:** 4–12 in. **Exposure:** Sun. **Water:** Regular. **Soil:** Adaptable.

This delightful, small annual features bright yellow flower heads. It blooms from March to May and is a nectar source for the endangered checkerspot butterfly. Goldfields are stunning planted in masses, and they are natural companions for tidy tips.

*Lasthenia californica*, goldfields

---

***Layia platyglossa*** **Tidy tips**

Asteraceae (Sunflower Family)

**Distribution:** Coastal bluffs and grasslands from Mendocino County to Baja California. **Height:** 6–24 in. **Spread:** 6–24 in. **Exposure:** Sun. **Water:** Moderate. **Soil:** Well-drained preferred.

Tidy tips, with their large, yellow, white-tipped daisy flowers, can be found in many parts of the state. *Platyglossa* means "wide tongue," which describes the wide petals of the ray flowers surrounding the central disk

*Layia platyglossa*, tidy tips

flowers. Narrow leaves, stems, and flower bracts are covered with short hairs and have a delicate fragrance. Tidy tips are easy to grow and bloom from March to June. At the end of summer, birds are apt to devour all of the seed unless it is protected. Plants must have sun and quite lean soil or they become leggy and produce fewer flowers. They are outstanding combined with baby blue eyes, gilias, goldfields, and lupines.

---

***Limnanthes douglasii*** **Meadowfoam**

Lentibulariaceae (Bladderwort Family)

**Distribution:** Grasslands and vernal pools of the inner Coast Ranges. **Height:** 6–12 in. **Spread:** 6–12 in. **Exposure:** Sun. **Water:** Moderate to regular. **Soil:** Adaptable, heavy preferred.

Meadowfoam is an enchanting annual that produces masses of bright yellow flowers with white tips. Plants are adaptable to garden conditions and self-sow in seasonally moist areas. They bloom in spring until the soil dries out, and they are ideal for containers.

*Limnanthes douglasii,* meadowfoam

***Limnanthes alba*** **White meadowfoam**

This is a delightful white-flowering annual, growing eight to twelve inches tall. It is found near vernal pools and seeps, but it adapts to garden conditions and re-seeds freely.

### *Linanthus grandiflorus* — Grand linanthus

Polemoniaceae (Phlox Family)

**Distribution:** Dry slopes in the Coast Ranges of northern and central California. **Height:** 6–24 in. **Spread:** 1 ft. **Exposure:** Sun or partial shade. **Water:** Occasional. **Soil:** Well-drained preferred.

Grand linanthus usually occurs in drifts or in masses, and it is often planted densely for its carpet of soft pink or white phloxlike flowers. Popular for its dainty aspect and clear, pastel colors, this species will bloom from spring to mid-summer with occasional irrigation. It is a good choice for rock gardens or dry slopes.

## *LUPINUS* SPECIES (LUPINES)

Fabaceae (Pea Family)

The experience of walking through sky-blue pools of fragrant lupines is unforgettable. They are a prominent feature of open fields, rolling hills, and coastal plains. Sometimes lupines are the dominant plant and cast a blue haze over the landscape, but in most places they mingle with other spring wildflowers. The classic combination of blue lupines and golden poppies is easy to replicate in a native garden.

*Lupinus* is a large genus with about thirty species of annuals. Flowers are arranged in whorls around the stem and have characteristics typical of the pea family. Leaves are palmately divided, green to gray-green, and hairy or smooth. Seeds of most annual lupines germinate readily. As a rule, lupines do not respond well to handling, but they may be started in flats or pots if transplanted when small. All species prefer full sun, lean soil, and water to supplement the spring rains.

*Lupinus bicolor*, miniature lupine

*Lupinus bicolor*, miniature lupine

*Lupinus nanus*, sky lupine

**TABLE 12.** *Lupinus* (Lupines)

| Plant | Distribution | Height | Spread |
|---|---|---|---|
| *L. bicolor* (miniature lupine), plate, figure | Grasslands, foothills, coastal regions | 4–16 in. | 6–20 in. |
| *L. densiflorus* (gully lupine) | Fields, hills, Santa Clara to Humbolt Cos. | 6–12 in. | 6–20 in. |
| *L. nanus* (sky lupine), plate | Grasslands and coastal scrub, widespread | 6–24 in. | 6–24 in. |
| *L. succulentus* (arroyo lupine) | Grasslands, Coast Ranges to Baja Cal. | 3 ft | 3 ft |

### ***Madia elegans*** — **Tarweed**

Asteraceae (Sunflower Family)

**Distribution:** Widespread in dry slopes and grasslands. **Height:** 4–6 ft. **Spread:** 4 ft. **Exposure:** Sun to partial shade. **Water:** Drought-tolerant to occasional. **Soil:** Adaptable.

This stunning annual blooms through the summer. Yellow, daisylike flowers with deep orange spots at the base of their petals, open at dusk and wilt during the day. Plants have a pungent aroma that comes from sticky glands covering the stems, leaves, and flower buds. Tarweeds are ideal for meadow gardens, and they provide food for butterflies and birds.

### ***Mentzelia lindleyi*** — **Blazing star**

Loasaceae (Loasa Family)

**Distribution:** Rocky slopes in coast sage scrub and oak and pine woodland, inner South Coast Ranges, Bay Area, and Central Valley. **Height:** 6–24 in. **Spread:** 6–24 in. **Exposure:** Sun. **Water:** Drought-tolerant to occasional. **Soil:** Well-drained.

Blazing star has long been used in gardens, and it tolerates water during its period of active growth. Saucer-shaped flowers are bright yellow with a red-orange center and conspicuous stamens. The petals are silky and rem-

| Flowers | Culture | Comments |
|---|---|---|
| Blue and white, March–May | Sun, semi-dry | Good massed |
| White, lilac, pink, blue, violet, April–June | Sun, semi-dry | Good color selection |
| Rich blue, white spots, April–May | Sun, semi-dry | Combine with Cal. poppies |
| Blue-purple, early spring | Sun | Good with grasses, larval food plant |

iniscent of California poppies. Foliage is lanceolate with narrow divisions, like a stiff fern. Blazing star is especially valuable with chia (*Salvia columbariae*) and other plants with blue flowers. Several lupines and penstemons also make good companions.

*Mentzelia lindleyi*, blazing star

## *NEMOPHILA* SPECIES (NEMOPHILAS)

Hydrophyllaceae (Waterleaf Family)

Nemophilas have long been favorite garden plants. Solitary, bowl-shaped flowers appear in several shades of blue and in white, sometimes with contrasting spots. Pale green foliage is pinnately divided and hairy. Nemophilas are often combined with bulbs and other annuals. Species of nemophila are easily grown from seed broadcast in autumn, and seeds may be sown again in early spring for a late bloom. Most will volunteer abundantly when allowed to go to seed. They may be used in many garden situations, especially with other annuals or in colonies among other plants. In the wild, nemophilas are an admirable feature of many oak woodlands and north-facing slopes.

**Distribution:** Moist slopes and meadows. **Height:** 4–6 in. **Spread:** 8–12 in. **Exposure:** Sun to partial shade. **Water:** Regular. **Soil:** Adaptable.

### *Nemophila maculata* — **Fivespot**

Native to moist places on the western slopes on the Sierra Nevada, fivespot has white flowers with a purple spot at the tip of each petal. It makes a pleasing combination with irises and early-flowering brodiaeas.

*Nemophila maculata*, fivespot

***Nemophila menziesii*** **Baby blue eyes**

This delightful wildflower heralds the beginning of spring. It can be found in the inner Coast Ranges and the Sierra foothills. Often used as a bulb cover, baby blue eyes has clear blue flowers with white centers. It is especially handsome with tufted poppy for the contrast of its clear, yellow flowers.

*Nemophila menziesii*, baby blue eyes

**_Phacelia tanacetifolia_** **Tansy-leaf phacelia**
Hydrophyllaceae (Waterleaf Family)

**Distribution:** Open areas in Central Valley and foothills from Lake County to Baja California. **Height:** 1–4 ft. **Spread:** 1–4 ft. **Exposure:** Sun or shade. **Water:** Drought-tolerant. **Soil:** Adaptable.

This fragrant annual is easy to grow and can be used in a mixture of hardy natives for informal areas of a garden. Tansy-leaf phacelia has also been used in agriculture as a cover crop or planted with field crops to attract beneficial insects. Abundant, bright blue flowers are coiled and have a fuzzy effect.

**_Phacelia minor_** **California bells**

This free-flowering species makes a lively splash of color in a sunny rock garden. Flowers are purple, in cymes, and foliage is dark green. California bells are common from the Santa Monica Mountains to the edge of the desert. They are not cold hardy and should not be planted where spring frosts are expected.

**_Phacelia viscida_** **Sticky phacelia**

This species is found in coastal scrub and chaparral from Monterey to San Diego counties. It is easy to grow in full sun and features vivid blue flowers with white centers.

**_Platystemon californicus_** **Cream cups**
Papaveraceae (Poppy Family)

**Distribution:** Widespread in grasslands, chaparral, and oak woodlands. **Height:** 4–8 in. **Spread:** 4–8 in. **Exposure:** Sun to partial shade. **Water:** Occasional. **Soil:** Adaptable.

All who love small plants are intrigued by this attractive annual. A member of the poppy family, it has cream-colored flowers that open from pendant, downy buds and glow when backlit. Leaves are pale green, linear, and hairy. Cream cups bloom from March to May and perform best in full sun with moderate amounts of water. Plants may be grown from seed, broadcast and raked in before the winter rains begin. They are known to seed abundantly in burn areas and in cultivated fields. Several native an-

*Platystemon californicus*, cream cups

nuals make suitable companions, including gilias, baby blue eyes, and Chinese houses.

---

### ***Salvia columbariae*** — **Chia**

Limiaceae (Mint Family)

**Distribution:** Common in coastal sage scrub and chaparral from inner Mendocino County to Baja California. **Height:** 6–24 in. **Spread:** 6–24 in. **Exposure:** Sun. **Water:** Drought-tolerant to occasional. **Soil:** Adaptable, well-drained preferred.

*Salvia columbariae*, chia

This fragrant wildflower produces several tiers of dark blue flowers. It blooms from March to June and is excellent with other sun-loving annuals and drought-tolerant perennials. The leaves are mostly basal with a rough texture, and the foliage resembles a thick, gray-green fern. This annual was one of the most important seed plants for the California Indians. They gathered the nutritious seeds in great quantities and ground them into meal for pinole. The Spanish settlers used the seeds, flavored with sugar or lemon, for a refreshing drink.

---

### *Stylomecon heterophylla* — Wind poppy

Papaveraceae (Poppy Family)

**Distribution:** Chaparral and grasslands, Coast Ranges, San Joaquin Valley, foothills of southern Sierra to Baja California. **Height:** 1–2 ft. **Spread:** 1–2 ft. **Exposure:** Sun to partial shade. **Water:** Drought-tolerant to occasional. **Soil:** Adaptable, well-drained preferred.

Wind poppy is admired for its delicate, orange-red flowers that are held on thin stalks above finely divided basal leaves. The flowers open from nodding buds, and there is a purple spot at the base of each flat petal. Soon after opening, the petals drop off. Although this lovely wildflower is ephemeral, and not entirely dependable as a garden plant, it is worth growing for its brilliantly colored flowers.

*Stylomecon heterophylla*, wind poppy

# BULBS

California's native bulbs have drawn admiration from the earliest explorers to present-day enthusiasts. They are the jewels of the native flora, with an impressive diversity and range. Members of the genus *Calochortus* are exquisite in every detail, wild onions and brodiaeas are admired for their rich colors, fawn lilies and fritillaries have endearing charms, and the true lilies are among the most elegant flowers to be found anywhere. Some species are exceedingly rare and restricted to specific environmental conditions, while others are widely distributed over the state. Native bulbs grow in a variety of habitats, including woodlands, moist meadows, and dry fields, where some occur in amazing quantities.

The abundance of some species may soon be only a memory as land development takes its toll on the native flora. Many bulbs produce offsets, but most species increase only from seed, and where their natural habitat has been disturbed, seedlings do not have the opportunity to reach maturity. Thus, some rare bulbs are in danger of becoming extinct. Three to five years, or sometimes longer, are required from seed to maturity, and disturbance during these critical years may cause young seedlings to die. There is still more to be learned about how best to protect, propagate, and grow native bulbs.

Successful cultivation of bulbs requires an understanding of their natural habitats, including the type of soil, the amounts of light and shade, and moisture levels. Most species require sharply drained soil and a summer dry period, but a few, like the true lilies, may be watered throughout the year. The growing cycle begins in autumn with the rains, and that is the best time to plant native bulbs. Flowering depends on sufficient moisture during the rainy season, and occasional irrigation may be required during dry spells. Planting bulbs in containers or raised beds makes is easier to control watering and protect them from gophers, rodents, deer, and other creatures. Pots of bulbs can be set into the ground in winter, their rims concealed with a light layer of mulch, and moved to a cool, dry place after flowering.

The native bulbs described in this chapter are adaptable to cultivation, and they can be found at specialty nurseries and botanic garden plant sales. Rare species should be left intact, and steps should be taken to preserve their native habitats so that all may enjoy these treasures of the California flora for years to come.

## *ALLIUM* SPECIES (WILD ONIONS)

Liliaceae (Lily Family)

Onions grow from small corms, each one tunicated with a different design and pattern. Flowers are in umbels of varying sizes that rise above the plant on leafless stalks, and colors range through shades of pink, rose, and purple or white. Foliage is basal, linear, and grass-like. Most wild onions grow in dry, open foothills or mountain regions, although some are native to meadows and moist fields. The native habitat of each must be kept in mind when they are planted in gardens. The species I have grown have been dependable and quite persistent when given the correct conditions. They perform well in colonies among hardy perennials and in meadows with native grasses and other wild bulbs. Onions have long been used as flavoring for food, and they were enjoyed by the California Indians.

### *Allium serratum* — Serrated onion

**Distribution:** Slopes and serpentine, Lake to Merced counties. **Height:** 8–16 in. **Exposure:** Sun. **Water:** Drought-tolerant. **Soil:** Adaptable, well-drained preferred.

Serrated onion produces dense, rose-pink umbels from March to May. It can be paired with brodiaea and other species with similar cultural requirements in rock gardens or dry borders.

*Allium serratum*, serrated onion

## *Allium unifolium* — Single leaf onion

**Distribution:** Moist, heavy soil, in chaparral and woodlands, Del Norte to Monterey counties. **Height:** 12–24 in. **Exposure:** Sun to partial shade. **Water:** Occasional to moderate. **Soil:** Adaptable.

Single leaf onion produces attractive lavender, pink, or white flowers in late spring and abundant seedlings. This adaptable species is easy to grow and tolerates clay soil and summer irrigation.

*Allium unifolium*, single leaf onion

## *BRODIAEA* SPECIES (BRODIAEAS)

Liliaceae (Lily Family)

The genus *Brodiaea* is concentrated in the Pacific states and is highly developed in California west of the Sierra Nevada. Many used to be so abundant that they covered California's hills and valleys with tints of blue and purple. Most are adaptable to garden cultivation, and they are eye-catching in a meadow with native grasses. Each flower is composed of six perianth segments fused at the base to form a tube. The segments expand into open, bell-shaped flowers on slender, smooth stems. All species have similar, grass-like foliage, generally sparse, and they grow from underground corms that store moisture and nutrients during the dormant season, usually summer and fall.

Plants with the genus names *Brodiaea, Dichelostemma,* and *Triteleia* are similar and were formerly in the genus *Bodiaea.* Members of the lily family, all have clusters of flowers with flower parts (petals, sepals, stamens) in threes or multiples of three. Brodiaeas are long-lived in a semi-dry situation. They have long been used in gardens and are easy to grow.

### *Brodiaea elegans* — Harvest brodiaea

**Distribution:** Heavy soils, grasslands, and open woods from Monterey County to Oregon. **Height:** 6–18 in. **Exposure:** Sun to partial shade. **Water:** Occasional to moderate. **Soil:** Adaptable.

Harvest brodiaea lights up meadows in Central California from May to July with open umbels of vivid blue-purple flowers. Multiplying well from year to year, it grows well in clay soils and in containers.

*Brodiaea elegans*, harvest brodiaea

## *Brodiaea californica* — California brodiaea

California brodiaea plant has erect umbels of lilac flowers that bloom from May to July on stems up to two feet tall. Native to open meadows and woodlands in Northern California, it prefers semi-dry conditions in lean soil.

*Brodiaea californica*, California brodiaea

## *CALOCHORTUS* SPECIES (MARIPOSA LILIES, FAIRY LANTERNS)

Liliaceae (Lily Family)

*Calochortus* are among the most rare and beautiful bulb plants in the world. Their exquisite beauty comes from a graceful bearing, shapely flowers, and intricate designs. Plants grow from a slender, coated corm, the coating varying from a thin, onion-like covering to ones of more fibrous texture. In all species, the flowers are composed of three petals and three sepals, on plants which may bear one or several blossoms. Most species bloom in spring or early summer and require dry summers. Foliage is thin and grass-like. Some find it easier to grow these bulbs in pots, using a friable soil mixture and allowing the pots to dry out after the foliage has died down.

Mariposa lilies have bowl-shaped flowers with the rim of the petals often rolled outward. Designs within the flowers consist of distinctive markings and spots, especially pronounced in white mariposa lily. Glands in the lower part of the flowers are generally fringed with hairs of similar or contrasting colors.

Fairy lanterns, also called globe tulips, produce lovely, pendant flowers formed of three petals turned inward, forming a globe, subtended by three shorter sepals. They are dainty and unexcelled for shade borders where their flowers will show to advantage. Globe tulips are more adaptable than mariposa lilies and may be used in lightly shaded borders where water is given for most of the year.

### *Calochortus albus* — White fairy lantern

**Distribution:** Widespread in foothills and open slopes in many plant communities. **Height:** 1–2 ft. **Exposure:** Sun to partial shade. **Water:** Drought-tolerant to moderate. **Soil:** Adaptable.

White fairy lantern has nodding, white or pink flowers on one- to two-foot stalks. This adaptable species is widespread in shaded areas, and it is lovely with irises and ferns in a woodland garden.

*Calochortus albus*, white fairy lantern

***Calochortus luteus*** **Yellow mariposa lily**

Yellow mariposa lily blooms from April to June. Flowers are yellow with reddish markings are held on stalks that grow up to twenty inches. It pairs well with brodiaeas or blue-eyed grass in a sunny, dry garden.

*Calochortus luteus*, yellow mariposa lily

***Calochortus venustus*** **White mariposa lily**

This lily has beautiful white, yellow, or pink flowers with intricate designs. The flower stalks are variable in height and produce up to six flowers that bloom from May to July. Mariposa lily is easy to grow, tolerates heavy clay soil, and combines well with other drought-tolerant natives.

---

***Chlorogalum pomeridianum*** **Soap plant**

Liliaceae (Lily Family)

**Distribution:** Dry hills, plains, and open woodlands throughout California. **Height:** foliage to 2 ft. Spread: 3 ft. **Exposure:** Sun to partial shade. **Water:** Drought-tolerant to occasional. **Soil:** Adaptable.

Soap plant is conspicuous for its long, tough, wavy-margined leaves and for widely branched inflorescences, bearing small white flowers with pink or purple veins, and opening in the evening. Flower stalks, rising four to six feet above the foliage, have an airy effect. Plants grow from a large bulb with a coarse, fibrous coating and are easy to cultivate. Volunteers often occur around established plants, creating open colonies of soap plant in the wild and in gardens. I have found this plant to be an interesting addition to a border of native shrubs and large perennials of similar requirements. Suitable for an oak woodland or open meadow, soap plant might be grown for its historical significance alone. There is a long list of Indian uses for this plant, including soap, food, fiber, and glue. The fibrous bulb coating was made into brushes, and crushed bulbs were used for stupefying fish.

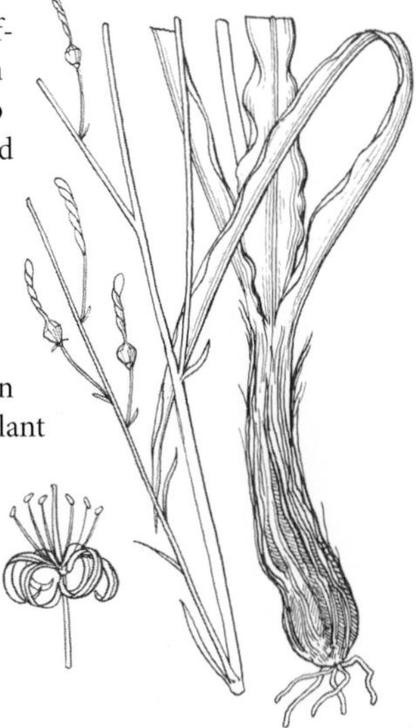

---

### *Dichelostemma capitatum* — Blue dicks

Liliaceae (Lily Family)

**Distribution:** Common in hills and valleys west of the Sierra Nevada. **Height:** 1–2 ft. **Exposure:** Sun to partial shade. **Water:** Drought-tolerant to moderate. **Soil:** Adaptable.

*Dichelostemma capitatum*, blue dicks

Blue dicks are found throughout California growing in dry fields with native grasses. Dense heads of blue-violet flowers, occasionally white or pink, bloom from March to May on slender stalks up to three feet tall. The leaves have often dried up and disappeared by the time the flowers open. Blue dicks increase by offsets and naturalize in gardens.

**_Dichelostemma ida-maia_** **Firecracker flower**

Firecracker flower produces clusters of narrow, cylindrical, crimson-red flowers with green tips and grows up to twenty inches tall. Native to meadows and forest edges in northern California, this colorful wildflower tolerates light shade and some summer moisture.

*Dichelostemma ida-maia*, firecracker flower

**_Erythronium californicum_** **Fawn lily**

Liliaceae (Lily Family)

**Distribution:** Woodlands from Colusa to Humboldt counties. **Height:** 8–16 in. **Exposure:** Partial shade. **Water:** Moderate. **Soil:** Well-drained preferred.

Fawn lily is admired for its charming white flowers, each with a pale yellow center. It blooms in early spring, and once established it is likely to flower with increasing abundance for many years. Marjorie Schmidt noted that fawn lilies planted under a live oak tree in her Los Gatos garden produced stems bearing as many as five flowers each season. Plants grow from an elongated corm, which produces a pair of handsome, mottled leaves. This long-lived plant is adaptable to cultivation and tolerates irrigation. Fawn lily should be used where there is not too much competition from large plants.

***Fritillaria affinis*** **Checker-lily or mission bells**

Liliaceae (Lily Family)

**Distribution:** Woodlands and grasslands from San Francisco Bay northward. **Height:** 8–12 in. **Exposure:** Partial shade. **Water:** Moderate. **Soil:** Adaptable, well-drained preferred.

Checker-lily is an enchanting, spring-blooming bulb with nodding flowers and subdued colors. The bulb is composed of fleshy scales, and it produces an erect stem with narrow, sessile leaves arranged in a basal whorl or scattered along the stem. For the first few years, and often for a year or more between flowering cycles, only leaves are produced, and the patient gardener is rewarded with a flowering stalk in the third or fourth year. Flowers are cup-shaped and brownish-purple with yellow mottling. Plants may be watered during their period of active growth, but they need a summer dormant period with no irrigation. Checker-lily is desirable for a shaded garden, and it responds well when suitable conditions are provided.

*Fritillaria affinis*, checker-lily

## *LILIUM* SPECIES (LILIES)

Lily Family (Liliaceae)

Lilies are refined plants with stunningly beautiful flowers and fine bearing. A dozen species of lilies are native to California, growing in dry and moist habitats. All are handsome, refined plants suitable to garden culture. They have stout stems that grow from scaly bulbs, with foliage in whorls or scattered along the stems. Large flowers are formed of six perianth segments (identical petals and sepals), recurved in most species. The six stamens are conspicuous with large anthers, and the stigma is three-lobed. The two species described here will flourish under cultivation and persist for many years.

### *Lilium humboldtii* — **Humboldt lily**

**Distribution:** Chaparral and open woodlands in Northern and Central California. **Height:** 3–6 ft. **Exposure:** Sun to partial shade. **Water:** Drought-tolerant to moderate. **Soil:** Well-drained.

Humboldt lily has nodding orange flowers with maroon spots, resembling a Turk's cap. Deep green leaves are arranged in whorls along the stem. Adapted to California's Mediterranean climate, this bulb may rot with summer irrigation. California fescue and wood ferns make good companions in gardens with filtered shade.

## *Lilium pardalinum* — Leopard lily

**Distribution:** Moist places in many plant communities throughout California. **Height:** 3–8 ft. **Exposure:** Sun to partial shade. **Water:** Occasional to moderate. **Soil:** Adaptable, well-drained preferred.

Native to watercourses and meadows, leopard lily is outstanding in gardens with other moisture-loving plants. The recurved, pendant flowers are pale orange with maroon spots, shading to red at the tips of the perianth segments. Flowers can be more than four inches long, and the large anthers are red, orange, or yellow. Tall stalks bear up to thirty flowers in late spring or early summer and carry several whorls of long, narrow leaves. This vigorous lily soon forms large clumps that may be divided every four or five years.

*Lilium pardalinum*, leopard lily

**_Triteleia laxa_** **Ithuriel's spear**
Liliaceae (Lily Family)

**Distribution:** Heavy soils in many plant communities from Oregon to the Transverse Ranges. **Height:** 6–24 in. **Exposure:** Sun to partial shade. **Water:** Drought-tolerant to moderate. **Soil:** Adaptable.

Ithuriel's spear is easy to grow in a dry garden, and it will tolerate some summer water. Spring-blooming flowers in shades of purple and blue are trumpet-shaped and held on slender stalks above leaves that may be slender or wide. It is lovely combined with native grasses and in containers.

*Triteleia laxa*, Ithuriel's spear

**_Triteleia hyacinthina_** **White brodiaea**

**_Triteleia peduncularis_** **Long-rayed brodiaea**

These species are also beautiful and adaptable. Both have narrow leaves and graceful clusters of white flowers that are held on slender, flowering stems up to two feet high. They are native to seeps and other places with abundant moisture in spring that dry out in summer, but they resist rotting in gardens with summer irrigation.

# VINES

California has only a few native vines, and they are all deciduous. They can be used to frame an entry; to cover walls, fences, arbors, and pergolas; or as groundcovers. Some vines need to be supported and others cling with coiling tendrils. Most require training and occasional pruning to look their best. The species described here flourish under cultivation and persist for many years. Vines also provide food and cover for wildlife. They are notable for their foliage and flowers, and California grape has edible fruits.

## *Aristolochia californica* — Dutchman's pipe

Aristolochiaceae (Pipevine Family)

**Distribution:** Along streams in forests and woodlands below 2,000 ft, Coast Ranges, and Sierra foothills of northern California. **Height:** Up to 12 ft. **Exposure:** Partial shade to shade. **Water:** Drought-tolerant to moderate. **Soil:** Adaptable.

Dutchman's pipe

This rhizomatous vine with pale green, heart-shaped leaves is named for its unusual flowers, which resemble a Dutchman's pipe. The curved, tubular flowers are cream-colored with burgundy veins. Dutchman's pipe blooms in winter and spring before leafing out. Sometimes used as a ground cover, it is most effective trained along a fence or arbor where its flowers can be appreciated. This vine is a larval food source for the pipevine swallowtail butterfly.

Pipevine swallowtail caterpillar

## *Clematis lasiantha* **Chaparral clematis**

Ranunculaceae (Buttercup Family)

**Distribution:** Chaparral and woodlands below 6,000 ft from central California to Baja California. **Height:** 10–15 ft. **Exposure:** Sun to partial shade. **Water:** Drought-tolerant to occasional. **Soil:** Adaptable, well-drained preferred.

*Clematis lasiantha*, chaparral clematis

Chaparral clematis is a woody, deciduous vine that climbs over trees and shrubs in its native habitat. Masses of cream-colored flowers with long white stamens burst open in spring, and showy, plumed fruits make an appearance in summer and fall. Compound leaves have three to five toothed leaflets. Chaparral clematis will quickly cover a fence and any nearby shrub. Once a year, in early spring, some of the long vines may be pruned out and a few shortened for good flower production.

Chaparral clematis, seeds

### *Clematis ligusticifolia* **Virgin's bower**

This vine is similar to chaparral clematis with large clusters of creamy flowers, plumed seed heads, and five to seven leaflets. It grows throughout the state and forms bowers in protected canyons, often near streams. Virgin's bower thrives in shade with some moisture but also tolerates drier conditions. Planted with mountain mahogany, the feathery seeds of both species will complement each other.

---

### *Lonicera hispidula* **Pink chaparral honeysuckle**

Caprifoliaceae (Honeysuckle Family)

**Distribution:** Wooded hills and canyons below 2,500 ft in northern and central California. **Height:** 30–40 ft. **Exposure:** Partial shade. **Water:** Occasional. **Soil:** Adaptable.

Pink chaparral honeysuckle is a fast-growing, woody vine with paired leaves and light pink flowers. In late summer it produces scarlet berries that are enjoyed by birds. This deciduous vine will climb if given support or sprawl along the ground, and it can become invasive if not controlled. Stems become rope-like with age.

*Lonicera hispidula*, pink chaparral honeysuckle

---

### *Vitis californica* **California grape**

Vitaceae (Grape Family)

**Distribution:** Along rivers and streams throughout California. **Height:** 30–40 ft. **Exposure:** Sun or partial shade. **Water:** Occasional to moderate. **Soil:** Adaptable.

California grape is a fast-growing, deciduous vine with edible fruit that is grown for its colorful fall foliage. It climbs by tendrils and has large, green leaves with lobed margins that turn red or yellow in autumn. Spring flow-

*Vitis californica*, California grape

California grape, developing fruit

ers are small and inconspicuous, and clusters of small, sweet grapes mature in late summer, attracting birds. It can quickly cover a slope or fence, seeming to leap onto nearby trees and shrubs if not controlled. The older stems have shredding bark and are easy to prune. California grape will layer and root in moist soil.

**CULTIVARS** 'Roger's Red' is a vigorous selection that is considered to be a natural hybrid between the native California grape and the European wine grape, *Vitis vinifera*. The leaves turn brilliant red in autumn, making it is a worthy rival to poison oak (*Toxicodendron diversilobum*) without the potential for unpleasant consequences. 'Walker Ridge' has yellow to red fall color and grows slowly to ten feet, making it a good choice where space is limited or for a container.

*Vitis californica* 'Roger's Red', Roger's Red grape

# GRASSES

Native grasses were once widespread in California, and their diverse range of habitats suggests many possibilities for their use in gardens. They are striking as accents, in drifts of a single species, as a foundation for wildflower meadows, or weaving through perennials and shrubs. The appeal of grasses is derived from their naturalistic effects, subtle colors, and seasonal textures. Rustled by the wind, grasses add sound and movement to a native garden. They have the added advantage of being easy to grow, free of pests and diseases, and deer-resistant.

The grasses described in this chapter include members of the grass family (Poaceae) as well as the sedge (Cyperaceae) and rush (Juncaceae) families. The "true" grasses have hollow, cylindrical stems with nodes. Sedges have solid stems that are triangular in cross section without nodes, and rushes have cylindrical, solid stems without nodes. Their characteristics are captured by an old rhyme, "Sedges have edges and rushes are round; grasses are hollow and rush all around."

Grasses come in a variety of textures and colors, and many species change color over the growing season. Some have fine-textured leaves and delicate flower stalks, while others are bold and dramatic. Their flowers are wind-pollinated so they lack the bright colors that other plants have evolved to attract insects for pollination. Individual flowers are small and inconspicuous with variable inflorescences (flowering structures). The bracts (enclosed seeds) can be quite showy and have a luminous quality when backlit by the sun.

When selecting grasses, it is important to know whether they are spreading or clump-forming. Spreading grasses are a good choice for groundcovers and slopes with ample space to roam. Clumping types, or bunchgrasses, are recommended for mixed plantings and meadows in combination with annual and perennial wildflowers and bulbs. Many species are long-lived, and their fibrous roots are excellent for binding the soil. Most native grasses are adapted to deep soils, typically clays and silts.

A number of grasses are attractive throughout the year, and some are particularly stunning when dormant. Cool-season grasses, adapted to California's Mediterranean climate, typically begin their growth cycle with the rains, bloom in spring, then set seed and rest in summer. Warm-season grasses, mostly from inland areas and mountain regions, begin growing in summer and are mostly dormant in winter.

Little maintenance is required other than cutting plants back about once a year and removing thatch to promote new growth and reduce fire danger. The best time to renovate most grasses is usually in winter or early spring or just before their growing season. Some grasses and sedges may perform well for several years with only occasional grooming to remove old foliage.

Grasses can be propagated by division, from cuttings of rhizomes, or from seed. Seeds of cool-season grasses should be sown in fall and warm-season species in spring. Sowing seeds in pots or flats generally offers better results than sowing them in the ground to avoid competition from weeds. When plants have developed a good root system, they can be transplanted into the garden. Many grasses are fast-growing and will produce flowers and set seed the first year.

This chapter includes some of my favorite native grasses that are well-suited to California gardens. There are selections for coastal and inland areas, and gardeners are encouraged to experiment with creative combinations.

### *Aristida purpurea* — **Purple three-awn**

Poaceae (Grass Family)

**Distribution:** Coastal sage scrub and chaparral in southern California. **Height:** 1–2 ft. **Spread:** 1 ft. **Exposure:** Sun to partial shade. **Water:** Drought-tolerant to occasional. **Soil:** Adaptable. **Growth Cycle:** Warm season.

*Aristida purpurea*, purple three-awn

This attractive grass forms dense clumps of fine-textured leaves and showy flower spikes. Needlelike, three-segmented awns emerge with a purple cast and are effective at catching the light. Purple three-awn is lovely in a meadow or with shrubs and perennials in a dry garden. It grows easily from seed.

### *Bouteloua gracilis* — **Blue grama**

Poaceae (Grass Family)

**Distribution:** Dry rocky slopes and drainages in coastal scrub, woodlands, and pine forests in southern California. **Height:** 1 ft. **Spread:** 1–2 ft. **Exposure:** Sun. **Water:** Drought-tolerant to occasional. **Soil:** Adaptable. **Growth Cycle:** Warm season.

*Bouteloua gracilis*, blue grama

Blue grama forms dense tufts of narrow, gray-green leaves. In late spring and summer it produces inflorescences that rise a foot above the foliage and resemble small brushes, or eye lashes, held in a horizontal position at the tip of each stalk. In winter plants fade to a straw color. This versatile bunchgrass can be used as a meadow grass or as a fine-textured lawn with monthly mowing. It is also attractive in containers.

---

***Calamagrostis foliosa*** **Cape Mendocino reedgrass**

Poaceae (Grass Family)

**Distribution:** Coastal bluffs, scrub, and forests of northern California. **Height:** 1 ft. **Spread:** 2 ft. **Exposure:** Sun to partial shade. **Water:** Occasional to moderate. **Soil:** Adaptable. **Growth Cycle:** Cool season.

*Calamagrostis foliosa*, Cape Mendocino reedgrass

Cape Mendocino reedgrass is a beautiful tufted grass with gray-green leaves tinged with purple. Arching flower spikes emerge in spring. It is effective planted in drifts or as a single specimen where it can be admired for its elegant display. Plants can be renewed by removing thatch, and they usually need to be replaced after three or four years. This grass does best in coastal areas of central and northern California.

***Calamagrostis nutkaensis*** **Pacific reedgrass**

Pacific reedgrass is native to moist, coastal habitats of the Coast Ranges and San Francisco Bay Area. Growing up to four feet tall with arching leaves and narrow flower spikes, this bold bunchgrass appreciates some shade in inland gardens.

*Calamagrostis nutkaensis*, Pacific reedgrass

## *CAREX* SPECIES (SEDGES)

Cyperaceae (Sedge Family)

California has more than 100 species of sedges adapted to many habitats. Although generally found in moist areas, some species tolerate dry conditions. Sedges have many landscape uses and require little care. Native Americans used them for food, clothing, and shelter.

**Distribution:** Moist meadows and stream banks in coastal scrub, woodlands, and forests throughout California. **Exposure:** Sun to shade. **Water:** Occasional to regular. **Soil:** Adaptable.

### ***Carex pansa*** — **California meadow sedge**

California meadow sedge is native to coastal strands and spreads by rhizomes to form dense colonies. As a lawn substitute, it tolerates foot traffic, requires only occasional mowing, and thrives with regular to infrequent watering. For a large area it is best to start with small seedlings, and they will fill in quickly to make a dense groundcover about six inches tall.

### ***Carex praegracilis*** — **Dune sedge**

This species has similar characteristics and also grows to about six inches in height.

### ***Carex tumulicola*** — **Foothill sedge**

Foothill sedge tolerates sun and drought, but it looks better in shade with occasional irrigation. Native to meadows and woodlands in Northern California, this attractive, clumping sedge is often confused with *Carex divulsa*, an introduced non-native species that is more vigorous than the native sedge and commonly called Berkeley sedge. Foothill sedge has dense, evergreen foliage and grows to two feet with an equal spread. It is a good choice for massed plantings or along paths or stream banks. Cutting plants back once a year improves its appearance.

*Carex tumulicola*, foothill sedge

## *Danthonia californica* — California oatgrass

Poaceae (Grass Family)

**Distribution:** Open meadows and forests in mountains and Coast Ranges. **Height:** 18 in. **Spread:** 1 ft. **Exposure:** Sun or partial shade. **Water:** Occasional. **Growth Cycle:** Cool season.

California oatgrass forms dense leafy tufts with nodding flower spikes and performs best in the coastal regions of central and northern California. It tolerates trampling and foot traffic, making it useful for mowed meadows. It can also be used in openings between shrubs and for erosion control on slopes. Plants grow easily from seed or by division, and they will self-sow.

*Danthonia californica*, California oatgrass

**_Deschampsia cespitosa_** **Tufted hairgrass**

Poaceae (Grass Family)

**Distribution:** Widely distributed in meadows, woodlands, and forests. **Height:** 1–2 ft. **Spread:** 2 ft. **Exposure:** Sun or shade. **Water:** Moderate to regular. **Soil:** Adaptable. **Growth Cycle:** Cool season.

Tufted hairgrass has dark green leaves and showy, golden panicles from spring into summer. Suited to moist places with partial shade, this grass is a good choice for massed plantings. It will self-sow in irrigated soil, and older plants can be replaced by seedlings every few years.

### *Deschampsia cespitosa* ssp. *holciformis*

This is a lower growing subspecies native to coastal prairies in Northern California. Inland it needs some shade and summer water. The cultivar 'Jughandle' is a dense bunchgrass with showy inflorescences.

*Deschampsia cespitosa* ssp. *holciformis*, tufted hairgrass

*Deschampsia cespitosa* ssp. *holciformis* 'Jughandle'

***Elymus glaucus*** **Blue wild rye**

Poaceae (Grass Family)

**Distribution:** Wide distribution in open areas and dry hills at mid-elevation. **Height:** 1 ft. **Spread:** 1–2 ft. **Exposure:** Sun. **Water:** Occasional to moderate. **Soil:** Adaptable. **Growth Cycle:** Cool season.

Blue wild rye is an attractive and reliable bunchgrass that can be used as a garden accent, in large-scale plantings, or on slopes for erosion control. It resembles *Muhlenbergia rigens*, but its smaller scale makes it useful for many garden situations. Slender flower spikes, erect and slightly arching, appear in spring and rise two to three feet above the foliage. Narrow leaves are green to gray-green. Blue wild rye is easy to propagate from seed or by division, and it often self-sows. Plants can be cut back in winter or early spring for renewal, and they will tolerate summer watering or drought. *Elymus glaucus* has sometimes been confused with *Leymus mollis*, a spreading grass with gray leaves. Blue wild rye can be combined with monkeyflowers, sages, and annual wildflowers for pleasing effects.

***Festuca californica*** **California fescue**

Poaceae (Grass Family)

**Distribution:** Open and wooded slopes in grasslands, chaparral, and open woodlands of northern California. **Height:** 2–3 ft. **Spread:** 2–3 ft. **Exposure:** Sun to partial shade. **Water:** Drought-tolerant to moderate. **Soil:** Adaptable. **Growth Cycle:** Cool season.

*Festuca californica*, California fescue

California fescue is admired for its attractive, arching flower stalks and handsome green to blue-gray foliage. This evergreen bunchgrass is long-lived and useful in many garden situations. It has a cascading effect when planted on slopes, and it does well with ferns and irises in a woodland setting. Supplemental irrigation and light shade are recommended away from the coast. Occasional grooming improves its appearance, and plants can be cut back in winter to stimulate new growth. There are several outstanding selections with blue-gray foliage.

**CULTIVARS** 'Blue Fountain', a Nevin Smith introduction, forms a compact clump of blue-gray foliage with flower spikes to about four feet. 'Horse Mountain Green' has leaves that are green with gray-green undersides and inflorescences rising to three feet. 'Phil's Silver', a selection from Phil Van Soelen, has graceful gray-green foliage that turns silver-gray in the dry season. 'Serpentine Blue' is an excellent blue-gray selection from Roger Raiche.

---

### ***Festuca idahoensis*** — **Idaho fescue**

Native to open woodlands and rocky slopes in northern California, Idaho fescue forms dense tufts of fine-textured, blue-green or gray-green leaves up to one foot tall with narrow panicles. This cool-season species prefers well-drained soil with sun or partial shade. It is lovely in drifts or in meadows with foothill penstemon and blue-eyed grass.

*Festuca idahoensis*, Idaho fescue

### ***Festuca rubra*** — **Red fescue**

This fine-textured fescue grows in moist, open places from the Coast Ranges to the Sierra. It spreads slowly by rhizomes to form a tufted carpet up to one foot high with flower stalks rising a foot above the foliage. Red fescue is an excellent choice for a moist meadow or a naturalistic lawn and can be mowed occasionally.

*Festuca rubra*, red fescue

***Juncus patens*** **California gray rush or common rush**

Juncaceae (Rush Family)

**Distribution:** Moist places in many plant communities from Baja California to Oregon. **Height:** 18–30 in. **Spread:** 1–2 ft. **Exposure:** Sun to partial shade. **Water:** Drought-tolerant to regular. **Soil:** Adaptable.

California gray rush forms clumps of wiry, upright, gray-green stems. This tough, adaptable plant prefers some summer water, although it also grows well in dry conditions. It is ideal for pond margins, seasonal streams, and containers. This rush may self-sow in moist habitats.

***Leymus condensatus* 'Canyon Prince'** **Canyon Prince wild rye**

Poaceae (Grass Family)

**Distribution:** Coastal scrub on Prince Island, near San Miguel Island. **Height:** 3–4 ft. **Spread:** 3 ft. **Exposure:** Sun to partial shade. **Water:** Drought-tolerant to occasional. **Soil:** Adaptable. **Growth Cycle:** Cool season.

An introduction from the Santa Barbara Botanic Garden, Canyon Prince wild rye has striking, silver-blue leaves. It produces flower spikes in some situations, but its foliage is the main attraction. Spreading by rhizomes,

*Leymus condensatus* 'Canyon Prince', Canyon Prince wild rye

this perennial grass is recommended for large gardens and slopes. The foliage can be cut back to the ground every few years when thatch accumulates to rejuvenate this handsome grass.

### *Leymus condensatus* — Giant wild rye

*Leymus condensatus*, giant wild rye

Giant wild rye grows to twelve feet tall and is native to dry slopes in southern California. It needs plenty of room to spread and is best in larger gardens.

### *Melica imperfecta* **Coast melic**

Poaceae (Grass Family)

**Distribution:** Chaparral and open woodland in canyons and foothills from San Francisco Bay to Baja California and the central and southern Sierra. **Height:** 2 ft. **Spread:** 1 ft. **Exposure:** Sun to partial shade. **Water:** Drought-tolerant to occasional. **Soil:** Adaptable. **Growth Cycle:** Cool season.

Coast melic goes dormant in summer and returns quickly with winter rains. It has tufted foliage and narrow flower panicles that dry to a straw color in summer. This variable species combines well with wildflowers in a meadow garden. It prefers full sun in cooler climates and partial shade in southern California and warm inland areas.

*Melica imperfecta*, coast melic

### *Melica californica* **California melic**

Native to the oak woodlands and grasslands of the central and northern Coast Ranges, California melic grass is a drought-tolerant bunchgrass with bright green leaves. Narrow flower spikes rise one to two feet above clumps of basal foliage.

### *Melica torreyana* — Torrey's melic

Torrey's melic is a fine-textured, tufted grass native to chaparral and coniferous forests in central and northern California. It grows one to two feet tall with an equal spread. Dormant in summer, this refined, cool-season grass is long-lived and tolerant of dry shade. It is a good choice for planting under oaks.

---

### *Muhlenbergia rigens* — Deer grass or basket grass

Poaceae (Grass Family)

**Distribution:** Many plant communities statewide in valleys and canyons. **Height:** 3 ft. **Spread:** 3–4 ft. **Exposure:** Sun to partial shade. **Water:** Drought-tolerant to moderate. **Soil:** Adaptable. **Growth Cycle:** Warm season.

*Muhlenbergia rigens*, deer grass or basket grass

Deer grass is one of California's most enduring grasses, attractive in every season with its fountain-shaped form and blend of pale green and tawny tones. It forms large, dense clumps of narrow leaves and slender, arching flower stalks that rise above the foliage. Plants should be cut back every three or four years in late summer or fall and raked to remove thatch, and they will quickly start to produce new growth. Deer grass performs best in sun, although it will tolerate light shade. This grass is spectacular as a focal point or planted in drifts in a large garden. Deer sometimes rest among these grasses in my garden, and they have long been valued for Indian basketry.

## *NASELLA* SPECIES (NEEDLEGRASSES)

Poaceae (Grass Family)

California has three species of *Nasella*, all with graceful tufts of narrow, green leaves that turn a soft tawny color in summer when the soil dries out. Delicate inflorescences with long awns appear in late winter through early spring. Plants self-sow but are not invasive. They should be cut back or mowed when dormant. Needlegrasses are ideal for meadow gardens or for naturalizing on slopes.

**Distribution:** Grassland, chaparral, and open woodland in valleys and foothills throughout the state. **Height:** 2–3 ft. **Spread:** 2 ft. **Exposure:** Sun to partial shade. **Water:** Drought-tolerant to occasional. **Soil:** Adaptable. **Growth Cycle:** Cool season.

### *Nasella cernua* — Nodding needlegrass

Nodding needlegrass has elegant flower spikes and is lovely in a dry meadow with California poppies. It is native to grassland and chaparral in the Coast Ranges and in southern California.

### *Nasella lepida* — Foothill needlegrass

This species is more refined than *Nasella pulchra* and tolerates light shade. It is widespread in chaparral and oak woodlands.

*Nasella pulchra*, purple needlegrass

***Nasella pulchra*** **Purple needlegrass**

California's state grass is widely distributed throughout the state, and it was prevalent in California's grasslands before the arrival of the Europeans. Graceful flower stalks have a purple cast, turning silver when dormant. This adaptable grass is suitable for dry meadows and slopes, and it can be mowed when dormant.

***Sporobolus airoides*** **Alkali sacaton**
Poaceae (Grass Family)

**Distribution:** Vernally moist meadows, alkali sinks, and coastal scrub in central and southern California. **Height:** 2–3 ft. **Spread:** 2–3 ft. **Exposure:** Sun. **Water:** Drought-tolerant to moderate. **Soil:** Adaptable, tolerates alkaline conditions. **Growth Cycle:** Warm season.

Alkali sacaton merits greater use in gardens for its elegant displays. Graceful panicles, opening with a pink cast and fading to silver, rise above a mound of pale, gray-green foliage. This adaptable plant tolerates irrigation, drought, and a wide range of soils. It is lovely in a meadow planting with deer grass, annual wildflowers, and buckwheats. Plants can be cut back every two or three years.

*Sporobolus airoides*, alkali sacaton

# PLANT SELECTION GUIDE

The following lists group plants with similar garden requirements and those noted for some special feature or specific garden use. They are intended to help with decisions about garden planning and plant combinations. The plants listed are described in more detail in the plant chapters. These lists are far from complete, and other plants may be appropriate in some situations.

There are many variables—soils, microclimates, preferences, horticultural practices—to consider in planning a garden, and experimentation is encouraged to determine which plants will thrive in a particular situation. Most useful of the following lists are the situation categories from which the gardener may choose groupings of plants that are most likely to grow well together.

***Garden Requirements/Special Features:***

1. **Sun/Dry Situation**
2. **Sun/Water Situation**
3. **Shade/Dry Situation**
4. **Shade/Water Situation**
5. **Butterflies**
6. **Coastal Conditions**
7. **Container Plants**
8. **Deer-Resistant Plants**
9. **Espalier**
10. **Fall Color**
11. **Hedges, Screens, and Windbreaks**
12. **Hummingbirds**
13. **Lawn Alternatives**
14. **Meadows**
15. **Ornamental Fruits, Cones, and Seeds**
16. **Slopes and Erosion Control**
17. **Small Trees**
18. **Under Oaks**

Note: "Species" includes all species described in this book. Plus (+) indicates that the plant is tolerant of conditions beyond those of the category in which it is placed.

## 1. Sun/Dry Situation

***Trees***

- ☐ *Abies bracteata,* Santa Lucia fir
- ☐ *Aesculus californica*, buckeye
- ☐ *Arbutus menziesii*, madrone
- ☐ *Calocedrus decurrens*, incense cedar
- ☐ *Cupressus* species, cypresses
- ☐ *Juglans californica*, California black walnut
- ☐ *Lyonothamnus floribundus*, Catalina ironwood
- ☐ *Pinus* species, pines
- ☐ *Quercus agrifolia*, coast live oak
- ☐ *Quercus douglasii*, blue oak
- ☐ *Quercus engelmannii*, Engelmann oak
- ☐ *Quercus kelloggii*, black oak

***Shrubs***

- ☐ *Adenostoma fasciculatum*, chamise
- ☐ *Arctostaphylos* species, manzanitas+
- ☐ *Artemisia californica*, California sagebrush
- ☐ *Baccharis pilularis*, coyote brush
- ☐ *Berberis* species, barberries+
- ☐ *Carpenteria californica*, bush anemone+
- ☐ *Ceanothus* species, ceanothus
- ☐ *Cercis occidentalis*, redbud
- ☐ *Cercocarpus betuloides*, mountain mahogany
- ☐ *Cneoridium dumosum*, bushrue+
- ☐ *Comarostaphylis diversifolia*, summer holly
- ☐ *Dendromecon* species, bush poppies
- ☐ *Eriogonum* species, buckwheats
- ☐ *Fremontodendron californicum*, fremontia
- ☐ *Galvezia speciosa*, island snapdragon
- ☐ *Garrya elliptica*, coast silk-tassel+
- ☐ *Hesperoyucca whipplei*, Our Lord's candle
- ☐ *Heteromeles arbutifolia*, toyon
- ☐ *Keckiella cordifolia*, heart-leaf keckiella+
- ☐ *Lavatera assurgentiflora*, tree mallow
- ☐ *Prunus* species, wild cherries
- ☐ *Rhamnus* species, coffeeberries+
- ☐ *Rhus* species, sumacs
- ☐ *Ribes malvaceum*, chaparral currant
- ☐ *Simmondsia chinensis*, jojoba
- ☐ *Trichostema lanatum*, woolly blue curls

**Perennials**

- ☐ *Achillea millefolium*, yarrow
- ☐ *Armeria maritima*, sea thrift
- ☐ *Asclepias* species, milkweeds
- ☐ *Coreopsis gigantea*, giant coreopsis
- ☐ *Dudleya* species, dudleyas
- ☐ *Encelia californica*, California sunflower
- ☐ *Epilobium canum*, California fuchsia
- ☐ *Erigeron glaucus*, seaside daisy
- ☐ *Eriogonum* species, buckwheats
- ☐ *Eriophyllum confertiflorum*, golden yarrow
- ☐ *Grindelia* species, gum plants+
- ☐ *Lepechinia* species, pitcher sages
- ☐ *Lupinus albifrons*, silver bush lupine
- ☐ *Mimulus* species, monkeyflowers
- ☐ *Monardella* species, coyote mints
- ☐ *Penstemon* species, penstemons
- ☐ *Ranunculus californicus*, California buttercup
- ☐ *Romneya coulteri*, matilija poppy
- ☐ *Salvia* species, sages
- ☐ *Sedum spathulifolium*, sedum
- ☐ *Sidalcea malviflora*, checkerbloom
- ☐ *Sisyrinchium bellum*, blue-eyed grass
- ☐ *Solidago californica*, California goldenrod

**Annuals**

- ☐ *Clarkia* species, clarkias
- ☐ *Eschscholzia californica*, California poppy
- ☐ *Gilia tricolor*, bird's eye gilia
- ☐ *Layia platyglossa*, tidy tips
- ☐ *Linanthus grandiflorus*, grand linanthus
- ☐ *Lupinus* species, lupines
- ☐ *Madia elegans*, tarweed
- ☐ *Mentzelia lindleyi*, blazing star
- ☐ *Phacelia* species, phacelias
- ☐ *Platystamen californicus*, cream cups
- ☐ *Salvia columbariae*, chia
- ☐ *Stylomecon heterophylla*, wind poppy

**Bulbs**

- ☐ *Alliums erratum*, serrated onion
- ☐ *Brodiaea* species, brodiaeas
- ☐ *Chalochortus luteus*, yellow mariposa lily

- ☐ *Chalochortus venustus*, white mariposa lily
- ☐ *Triteleia laxa*, Ithuriel's spear

***Vines***

- ☐ *Clematis lasiantha*, chaparral clematis
- ☐ *Loncera hispidula*, pink chaparral honeysuckle

***Grasses***

- ☐ *Aristida purpurea*, purple three-awn
- ☐ *Bouteloua gracilis*, blue grama
- ☐ *Carex pansa*, California meadow sedge
- ☐ *Danthonia californica*, California oatgrass
- ☐ *Elymus glaucus*, blue wild rye
- ☐ *Festuca californica*, California fescue+
- ☐ *Festuca idahoensis*, Idaho fescue
- ☐ *Leymus condensatus* 'Canyon Prince', Canyon Prince wild rye
- ☐ *Melica imperfecta*, coast melic
- ☐ *Muhlenbergia rigens*, deer grass+
- ☐ *Nasella* species, needlegrasses
- ☐ *Sporobolus airoides*, alkali sacaton

## 2. Sun/Water Situation

***Trees***

- ☐ *Chamaecyparis lawsoniana*, Lawson cypress
- ☐ *Juglans californica*, California black walnut+
- ☐ *Platanus racemosa*, western sycamore
- ☐ *Populus fremontii*, Fremont cottonwood
- ☐ *Pseudotsuga menziesii*, Douglas fir
- ☐ *Quercus lobata*, valley oak
- ☐ *Sequoia sempervirens*, coast redwood
- ☐ *Sequoiadendron giganteum*, giant sequoia
- ☐ *Thuja plicata*, western red cedar

***Shrubs***

- ☐ *Arctostaphylos uva-ursi*, bearberry+
- ☐ *Cneoridium dumosum*, bushrue+
- ☐ *Keckiella cordifolia*, heart-leaf keckiella+
- ☐ *Philadelphus lewisii*, western mock orange
- ☐ *Ribes aureum*, golden currant
- ☐ *Rhododendron occidentale*, western azalea+

***Perennials***

- ☐ *Arabis blepharophylla*, rose rock cress
- ☐ *Erysimum concinnum*, Pt. Reyes wallflower+

- ☐ *Fragaria chiloensis*, beach strawberry
- ☐ *Grindelia* species, gum plants+
- ☐ *Sisyrinchium californicum*, yellow-eyed grass

**_Annuals_**

- ☐ *Lasthenia californica*, goldfields
- ☐ *Limnanthes douglasii*, meadowfoam
- ☐ *Nemophila* species, nemophilas

**_Bulbs_**

- ☐ *Allium unifolium*, single leaf onion

**_Grasses_**

- ☐ *Calamagrastis foliosa*, Cape Mendocino reedgrass
- ☐ *Calamagrostis nutkaensis*, Pacific reedgrass
- ☐ *Deschampsia cespitosa*, tufted hairgrass+
- ☐ *Festuca rubra*, red fescue
- ☐ *Juncus patens*, California gray rush+
- ☐ *Muhlenbergia rigens*, deer grass+

## 3. Shade/Dry Situation

**_Shrubs_**

- ☐ *Carpenteria californica*, bush anemone+
- ☐ *Garrya elliptica*, coast silk-tassel+
- ☐ *Rhamnus* species, coffeeberries+
- ☐ *Ribes indecorum*, white-flowered currant
- ☐ *Ribes speciosum*, fuchsia-flowered currant+
- ☐ *Rosa californica*, California wild rose
- ☐ *Styrax offficinalis redivivus*, snowdrop bush
- ☐ *Symphoricarpos* species, snowberries

**_Perennials_**

- ☐ *Iris* species, irises
- ☐ *Polystichum munitum*, western sword fern+
- ☐ *Salvia spathacea*, hummingbird sage
- ☐ *Satureja douglasii*, yerba buena

**_Bulbs_**

- ☐ *Chlorogalum pomeridianum*, soap plant
- ☐ *Fritillaria affinis*, checker-lily
- ☐ *Lilium humboldtii*, Humboldt lily

**_Vines_**

- ☐ *Clematis ligusticifolia*, virgin's bower

#### Grasses

- ☐ *Carex tumulicola*, foothill sedge
- ☐ *Festuca californica*, California fescue+
- ☐ *Juncus patens*, California gray rush+
- ☐ *Melica torreyana*, Torrey's melic

## 4. Shade/Water Situation

#### Trees

- ☐ *Acer species*, maples
- ☐ *Alnus rhombifolia*, white alder
- ☐ *Torreya californica*, California nutmeg
- ☐ *Umbellularia californica*, California bay

#### Shrubs

- ☐ *Arcstaphylos uva-ursi*, bearberry+
- ☐ *Artemisia douglasiana*, mugwort
- ☐ *Berberis aquifoilium*, Oregon grape
- ☐ *Berberis nervosa*, longleaf barberry
- ☐ *Calylcanthus occidentalis*, spice bush
- ☐ *Cornus sericea*, creek dogwood
- ☐ *Corylus cornuta* var. *californica*, California hazelnut
- ☐ *Gaultheria shallon*, salal
- ☐ *Holodiscus discolor*, cream bush
- ☐ *Myrica californica*, Pacific wax myrtle
- ☐ *Philadelphus lewisii*, western mock orange
- ☐ *Physocarpus capitatus*, ninebark
- ☐ *Rhododendron occidentale*, western azalea+
- ☐ *Ribes sanguineum* var, *glutinosum*, pink-flowering currant
- ☐ *Ribes speciosum*, fuchsia-flowered currant+
- ☐ *Vaccinium ovatum*, huckleberry

#### Perennials

- ☐ *Adiantum pedatum*, five-finger fern
- ☐ *Aquilegia formosa*, western columbine
- ☐ *Asarum caudatum*, wild ginger
- ☐ *Dicentra formosa*, western bleedingheart
- ☐ *Dodecatheon hendersonii*, Henderson's shooting star
- ☐ *Fragaria vesca*, woodland strawberry
- ☐ *Heuchera* species, coral bells
- ☐ *Oxalis oregana*, redwood sorrel
- ☐ *Polystichum munitum*, western sword fern+
- ☐ *Salvia spathacea*, hummingbird sage

- ☐ *Satureja douglasii*, yerba buena
- ☐ *Tellima grandiflora*, fringe cups
- ☐ *Vancouveria* species, inside-out flowers

***Annuals***

- ☐ *Clarkia concinna*, red ribbons clarkia
- ☐ *Claytonia perfoliata*, miner's lettuce
- ☐ *Collinsia heterophylla*, Chinese houses

***Bulbs***

- ☐ *Calochortus albus*, white fairy lantern
- ☐ *Erythronium californicum*, fawn lily
- ☐ *Lilium pardalinum*, leopard lily

***Vines***

- ☐ *Aristolochia californica*, Dutchman's pipe
- ☐ *Vitis californica*, California grape

***Grasses***

- ☐ *Deschampsia cespitosa*, tufted hairgrass+
- ☐ *Carex tumulicola*, foothill sedge

## 5. Butterflies

Nectar plants that attract butterflies are noted with *, and those noted with ** are both nectar plants and larval hosts.

- ☐ *Achillea millefolium***, yarrow
- ☐ *Aesculus californica**, California buckeye
- ☐ *Aristolochia californica*, Dutchman's pipe
- ☐ *Asclepias* species**, milkweeds
- ☐ *Baccharis pilularis**, coyote brush
- ☐ *Ceanothus* species*, ceanothus
- ☐ *Cercocarpus betuloides*, mountain mahogany
- ☐ *Encelia californica*, California sunflower
- ☐ *Eriogonum* species**, buckwheats
- ☐ *Grindelia* species, gum plants
- ☐ *Mimulus aurantiacus*, sticky monkeyflower
- ☐ *Monardella villosa**, coyote mint
- ☐ *Quercus* species, oaks
- ☐ *Rhamnus californica*, coffeeberry
- ☐ *Solidago californica**, California goldenrod

## 6. Coastal Conditions

These plants tolerate fog, wind, and salt air in coastal areas.

***Trees***

- ☐ *Cupressus macrocarpa*, Monterey Cypress
- ☐ *Pinus contorta*, beach pine
- ☐ *Pinus radiata*, Monterey pine
- ☐ *Pinus torreyana*, Torrey pine

***Shrubs***

- ☐ *Arctostaphylos edmundsii* 'Carmel Sur', Little Sur manzanita
- ☐ *Arctostaphylos* 'Emerald Carpet', emerald carpet manzanita
- ☐ *Arcstaphylos uva-ursi*, bearberry
- ☐ *Baccharis pilularis*, coyote brush
- ☐ *Ceanothus gloriosus*, Pt. Reyes ceanothus
- ☐ *Ceanothus griseus horizontalis*, Carmel creeper
- ☐ *Ceanothus thyrsiflorus*, blue blossom
- ☐ *Cneoridium dumosum*, bushrue
- ☐ *Eriogonum* species, buckwheats
- ☐ *Gaultheria shallon*, salal
- ☐ *Holodiscus discolor*, ocean spray
- ☐ *Lavatera assurgentiflora*, tree mallow
- ☐ *Myrica californica*, Pacific wax myrtle
- ☐ *Physocarpus capitatus*, ninebark
- ☐ *Rhamnus californica*, coffeeberry
- ☐ *Rhus integrifolia*, lemonade berry

***Perennials***

- ☐ *Achillea millefolium*, yarrow
- ☐ *Arabis blepharophylla*, rose rock cress
- ☐ *Armeria maritima*, sea thrift
- ☐ *Coreopsis gigantea*, giant coreopsis
- ☐ *Dudleya* species, liveforevers
- ☐ *Encelia californica*, California sunflower
- ☐ *Erigeron glaucus*, seaside daisy
- ☐ *Eriogonum* species, buckwheats
- ☐ *Eriophyllum nevinii*, Catalina silverlace
- ☐ *Erysimum concinnum*, Pt. Reyes wallflower
- ☐ *Fragaria chiloensis*, beach strawberry
- ☐ *Grindelia stricta* var. *platyphylla*, spreading gum plant
- ☐ *Heuchera* species, coral bells
- ☐ *Iris* species, irises
- ☐ *Lupinus arboreus*, yellow bush lupine

- ☐ *Mimulus* species, monkeyflowers
- ☐ *Salvia* species, sages
- ☐ *Satureja douglasii*, yerba buena
- ☐ *Sedum spathulifolium*, sedum
- ☐ *Sidalcea malviflora*, checkerbloom
- ☐ *Sisyrinchium* species, blue-eyed and yellow-eyed grass

#### Annuals

- ☐ *Eschscholzia californica*, California poppy

#### Grasses

- ☐ *Aristida purpurea*, purple three-awn
- ☐ *Calamagrostic* species, reedgrasses
- ☐ *Carex praegracilis*, dune sedge
- ☐ *Danthonia californica*, California oatgrass
- ☐ *Deschampsia cespitosa* ssp. *holciformis*, tufted hairgrass
- ☐ *Festuca rubra*, red fescue

## 7. Container Plants

Plants noted with * are suitable for large containers. Many annual wildflowers, perennials, bulbs, succulents, ferns, and grasses are ideal for containers, and they can be combined for interesting effects.

- ☐ *Acer circinatum**, vine maple
- ☐ *Adiantum pedatum*, five-finger fern
- ☐ *Arcstostaphylos uva-ursi*, bearberry
- ☐ *Armeria maritima*, sea thrift
- ☐ *Dudleya* species, dudleyas
- ☐ *Eriogonum species*, buckwheats
- ☐ *Garrya elliptica**, coast silk-tassel
- ☐ *Fragaria* species, strawberries
- ☐ *Heuchera* species, coral bells
- ☐ *Lewisia cotyledon*, cliff-maids
- ☐ *Monardella* species, coyote mints
- ☐ *Pinus contorta**, beach pine
- ☐ *Rhodendron occidentale*, western azalea
- ☐ *Ribes aureum**, golden current
- ☐ *Satureja douglasii*, yerba buena
- ☐ *Sedum spathulifolium*, sedum
- ☐ *Sisyrinchium bellum*, blue-eyed grass
- ☐ *Trichostema lanatum**, woolly blue curls
- ☐ *Vaccinium ovatum*, huckleberry

## 8. Deer-Resistant Plants

The following plants are generally not browsed by deer. Grasses, ferns, plants with aromatic foliage, and those with tough, prickly leaves are reliably deer-resistant.

#### Trees

Buckeyes and maples may need protection when young. Once established, most trees are deer-resistant.

#### Shrubs

- ☐ *Arctostaphylos* species, manzanitas
- ☐ *Artemisia* species, sagebrushes
- ☐ *Baccharis pilularis*, coyote brush
- ☐ *Berberis* species, barberries
- ☐ *Calycanthus occidentalis*, spice bush
- ☐ *Ceanothus* species, ceanothus (only species with small, prickly leaves)
- ☐ *Cercis occidentalis*, redbud
- ☐ *Cercocarpus betuloides*, mountain mahogany
- ☐ *Corylus cornuta*, hazelnut
- ☐ *Garrya elliptica*, coast silk-tassel
- ☐ *Hesperoyucca whipplei*, Our Lord's candle
- ☐ *Holodiscus discolor*, cream bush
- ☐ *Myrica californica*, Pacific wax myrtle
- ☐ *Rhamnus* species, coffeeberry and redberry
- ☐ *Rhus* species, lemonade berry, sugar bush
- ☐ *Ribes speciosum*, fuchsia-flowered gooseberry
- ☐ *Ribes viburnifolium*, Catalina perfume
- ☐ *Trichostema lanatum*, woolly blue curls
- ☐ *Vaccinium ovatum*, huckleberry

#### Perennials

- ☐ *Achillea millefolium*, yarrow
- ☐ *Asarum caudatum*, wild ginger
- ☐ *Asclepias* species, milkweeds
- ☐ *Epilobium canum*, California fuchsia
- ☐ *Erigeron glaucus*, seaside daisy
- ☐ *Eriogonum umbellatum*, sulfur buckwheat
- ☐ *Fragaria* species, strawberries
- ☐ *Iris* species, irises
- ☐ *Lepechinia* species, pitcher sages
- ☐ *Mimulus* species, monkeyflowers
- ☐ *Monardella* species, coyote mints
- ☐ *Penstemon* species, penstemons

- ☐ *Polystichum munitum*, western sword fern
- ☐ *Ranunculus californicus*, California buttercup
- ☐ *Romneya coulteri*, Matilija poppy
- ☐ *Salvia* species, sages
- ☐ *Satureja douglasii*, yerba buena
- ☐ *Sisyrinchium* species, blue-eyed and yellow-eyed grass
- ☐ *Solidago californica*, California goldenrod
- ☐ *Vancouveria planipetala*, inside-out flower
- ☐ *Woodwardia fimbriata*, giant chain fern

#### Annuals

- ☐ *Claytonia perfoiata*, miner's lettuce
- ☐ *Eschscholzia californica*, California poppy
- ☐ *Lupinus* species, lupines
- ☐ *Salvia columbariae*, chia

#### Bulbs

- ☐ *Allium* species, wild onions

#### Vines

- ☐ *Aristolochia californica*, Dutchman's pipe
- ☐ *Clematis* species, clematis
- ☐ *Lonicera hispidula*, pink chaparral honeysuckle

#### Grasses

All are deer-resistant.

## 9. Espalier

These plants can be trained against a wall or fence.

- ☐ *Arctostaphylos bakeri* 'Louis Edmunds', Louis Edmunds manzanita
- ☐ *Arctostaphylos densiflora* 'Sentinel', sentinel manzanita
- ☐ *Aristolochia californica*, Dutchman's pipe
- ☐ *Carpenteria californica*, bush anemone
- ☐ *Cercis occidentalis*, redbud
- ☐ *Clematis* species, clematis
- ☐ *Garrya elliptica*, coast silk-tassel
- ☐ *Heteromeles arbutifolia*, toyon
- ☐ *Lonicera hispidula*, pink chaparral honeysuckle
- ☐ *Rhamnus crocea*, redberry
- ☐ *Ribes aureum*, golden currant
- ☐ *Ribes speciosum*, fuchsia-flowered gooseberry
- ☐ *Rhus integrifolia*, lemonade berry
- ☐ *Vitis californica*, California grape

## 10. Fall Color

A number of plants have colorful autumn foliage. Many grasses have a luminous quality and colors that fade to brown, silver, and gold in late summer and fall.

- ☐ *Acer* species, maples
- ☐ *Berberis* aquifolium, Oregon grape
- ☐ Cercis occidentalis, redbud
- ☐ *Cornus sericea*, creek dogwood
- ☐ *Juglans californica*, California black walnut
- ☐ *Platanus racemosa*, California sycamore
- ☐ *Populus fremontii*, Fremont cottonwood
- ☐ *Quercus kelloggii*, black oak
- ☐ *Vitis californica*, California grape

## 11. Hedges, Screens, and Windbreaks

Plants noted with * are suitable for clipped hedges.

- ☐ *Arctostaphylos densiflora* 'Howard McMinn'*, Howard McMinn manzanita
- ☐ *Berberis aquifolium*, Oregon grape
- ☐ *Berberis nevinii*, Nevin's barberry
- ☐ *Ceanothus impressus*, Santa Barbara ceanothus
- ☐ *Ceanothus thyrsiflorus*, blue blossom
- ☐ *Chamaecyparis lawsoniana*, Lawson cypress
- ☐ *Comarostaphylos diversifolia*, summer holly
- ☐ *Cupressus* species*, cypresses
- ☐ *Garrya elliptica*, coast silk-tassel
- ☐ *Heteromeles arbutifolia*, toyon
- ☐ *Lavatera assurgentiflora*, tree mallow
- ☐ *Myrica californica*, Pacific wax myrtle
- ☐ *Prunus* species*, wild cherries
- ☐ *Rhamnus californica*, coffeeberry
- ☐ *Rhus integrifolia**, lemonade berry
- ☐ *Rhus ovata**, sugar bush
- ☐ *Ribes speciosum*, fuchsia-flowered gooseberry
- ☐ *Rosa californica*, California wild rose
- ☐ *Simmondsia chinensis*, jojoba
- ☐ *Umbellularia californica**, California bay

## 12. Hummingbirds

These plants attract hummingbirds.

- ☐ *Aquilegia formosa*, western columbine
- ☐ *Arbutus menziesii*, madrone
- ☐ *Arctostaphylos* species, manzanitas
- ☐ *Comarostaphylis diversifolia*, summer holly
- ☐ *Epilobium canum*, California fuchsia
- ☐ *Galvezia speciosa*, island snapdragon
- ☐ *Heuchera* species, coral bells
- ☐ *Lonicera hispidula*, pink chaparral honeysuckle
- ☐ *Mimulus* species, monkeyflowers
- ☐ *Penstemon* species, penstemons
- ☐ *Ribes* species, currants
- ☐ *Salvia* species, sages

## 13. Lawn Alternatives

There are many possibilities for using native grasses and other groundcovers as a substitute for conventional lawns. The plants noted with * are adapted to shade.

- ☐ *Achillea millefolium*, yarrow
- ☐ *Allium unifolium*, single leaf onion
- ☐ *Arcstaphylos* species, manzanitas (low forms)
- ☐ *Armeria maritima*, sea thrift
- ☐ *Asarum caudatum**, wild ginger
- ☐ *Baccharis pilularis* 'Twin Peaks', coyote brush
- ☐ *Berberis repens**, creeping barberry
- ☐ *Bouteluoa gracilis*, blue grama
- ☐ *Brodiaea* species, brodiaeas
- ☐ *Calamagrostis* species, reedgrasses
- ☐ *Carex pansa*, California meadow sedge
- ☐ *Carex praegracilis*, dune sedge
- ☐ *Ceanothus* 'Centennial', Centennial ceanothus
- ☐ *Ceanothus gloriosus* var. *porrectus**, Mt. Vision ceanothus
- ☐ *Ceanothus hearstiorum*, Hearst's ceanothus
- ☐ *Danthonia californica*, California oatgrass
- ☐ *Epilobium canum*, California fuchsia
- ☐ *Festuca rubra*, red fescue
- ☐ *Fragaria chiloensis*, beach strawberry
- ☐ *Fragaria vesca**, woodland strawberry
- ☐ *Nasella pulchra*, purple needlegrass
- ☐ *Rhamnus californica* 'Sea View', Sea View coffeeberry

- ☐ *Satureja douglasii**, yerba buena
- ☐ *Sisyrinchium* species, blue-eyed grass, yellow-eyed grass
- ☐ *Vancouveria* species*, inside-out flowers

## 14. Meadows

Grasses and grass-like plants provide a framework for wildflower meadows. A selection of annuals, perennials, and bulbs adapted to similar conditions can be planted between grasses.

#### *Dry Meadow*

- ☐ *Aristida purpurea*, purple three-awn
- ☐ *Bouteloua gracilis*, blue grama
- ☐ *Danthonia californica*, California oatgrass
- ☐ *Festuca californica*, California fescue
- ☐ *Festuca idahoensis*, Idaho fescue
- ☐ *Melica imperfecta*, coast melic
- ☐ *Nasella* species, needlegrasses
- ☐ *Sporobolus airoides*, alkali sacaton

#### *Moist Meadow*

- ☐ Calamagrostis foliosa, Cape Mendocino reedgrass
- ☐ *Calamagrostis nutkaensis*, Pacific reedgrass
- ☐ *Carex tumulicola*, foothill sedge
- ☐ *Deschampsia cespitosa*, tufted hairgrass
- ☐ *Festuca rubra*, red fescue

## 15. Ornamental Fruits, Cones, and Seeds

These plants have ornamental fruits, cones, and seeds for seasonal interest.

#### *Trees*

- ☐ *Abies bracteata*, Santa Lucia fir
- ☐ *Alnus rhombifoia*, white alder
- ☐ *Aesculus californica*, buckeye
- ☐ *Arbutus menziesii*, madrone
- ☐ *Calocedrus decurrens*, incense cedar
- ☐ *Cercis occidentalis*, redbud
- ☐ *Cupressus* species, cypresses
- ☐ *Pinus* species, pines
- ☐ *Quercus* species, oaks
- ☐ *Sequoia sempervirens*, coast redwood
- ☐ *Thuya plicata*, western red cedar
- ☐ *Torreya californica*, California nutmeg

#### *Shrubs*

- ☐ *Arctostaphylos species*, manzanitas
- ☐ *Berberis* species, barberries
- ☐ *Calycanthus occidentalis*, spice bush
- ☐ *Cercis occidentalis*, redbud
- ☐ *Cercocarpus betuliodes*, mountain mahogany
- ☐ *Comarostaphylis diversifolia*, summer holly
- ☐ *Garrya elliptica*, coast silk-tassel
- ☐ *Gaultheria shallon*, salal
- ☐ *Prunus* species, wild cherries
- ☐ *Rhamnus* species, coffeeberries
- ☐ *Rhus* species, sumacs
- ☐ *Ribes* species, currants
- ☐ *Symphoricarpos* species, snowberries

#### *Perennials*

- ☐ *Eriogonum* species, buckwheats
- ☐ *Salvia* species, sages

#### *Vines*

- ☐ *Clematis* species, clematis
- ☐ *Lonicera hispidula*, pink chaparral currant

#### *Grasses*

All have ornamental bracts or enclosed seeds.

## 16. Slopes and Erosion Control

These spreading and deep-rooted plants are recommended for slopes and erosion control.

- ☐ *Arctostaphylos hookeri*, Monterey manzanita
- ☐ *Arctostaphylos* 'Pacific Mist', Pacific mist manzanita
- ☐ *Baccharis pilularis*, coyote brush
- ☐ *Berberis aquifolium* 'Compacta', Oregon grape
- ☐ *Carex* species, sedges
- ☐ *Ceanothus* 'Centennial', centennial ceanothus
- ☐ *Ceanothus gloriosus*, Pt. Reyes ceanothus
- ☐ *Ceanothus griseus* var. *horizontalis*, Carmel creeper
- ☐ *Ceanothus maritimus*, maritime ceanothus
- ☐ *Danthonia californica*, California oatgrass
- ☐ *Elymus glaucus*, Blue wild rye
- ☐ *Encelia californica*, California sunflower
- ☐ *Epilobium canum*, California fuchsia
- ☐ *Festuca californica*, California fescue

- ☐ *Festuca rubra*, red fescue
- ☐ *Leymus condensatus* 'Canyon Prince', Canyon Prince wild rye
- ☐ *Muhlenbergia rigens*, deer grass
- ☐ *Nasella* species, needlegrasses
- ☐ *Physocarpus capitatus*, ninebark
- ☐ *Rhamnus californica*, coffeeberry
- ☐ *Ribes viburnifolium*, evergreen currant
- ☐ *Rhus integrifolia*, lemonade berry
- ☐ *Rhus ovata*, sugar bush
- ☐ *Rosa californica*, California wild rose
- ☐ *Salvia* 'Bee's Bliss', bee's bliss sage
- ☐ *Salvia leucophylla, purple sage*
- ☐ *Salvia sonomensis*, Sonoma sage
- ☐ *Salvia spathacea*, hummingbird sage
- ☐ *Solidago californica*, California goldenrod
- ☐ *Symphoricarpos species*, snowberries

## 17. Small Trees

Large shrubs that can become tree-like are indicated with *.

- ☐ *Acer circinatum*, vine maple
- ☐ *Aesculus californica*, California buckeye
- ☐ *Arctostaphylos manzanita* 'Dr. Hurd'*, Dr. Hurd manzanita
- ☐ *Chamaecyparis lawsoniana*, Lawson Cypress
- ☐ *Ceanothus arboreus**, Catalina ceanothus
- ☐ *Ceanothus* 'Ray Hartman'*, Ray Hartman ceanothus
- ☐ *Ceanothus thyrsiflorus**, blue blossom
- ☐ *Cercis occidentalis**, redbud
- ☐ *Cercocarpus betuloides**, mountain mahogany
- ☐ *Comarostaphylis diversifolia**, summer holly
- ☐ *Cupressus forbesii*, tecate Cypress
- ☐ *Garrya elliptica**, coast silk-tassel
- ☐ *Heteromeles arbutifolia**, toyon
- ☐ *Myrica californica**, Pacific wax myrtle
- ☐ *Pinus contorta*, beach pine
- ☐ *Prunus* species*, wild cherries
- ☐ *Rhus* species*, lemonade berry, sugar bush

## 18. Under Oaks

These plants tolerate dry shade under oaks.

- ☐ *Aquilegia formosa*, red columbine
- ☐ *Arctostaphylos hookeri* 'Wayside', Monterey manzanita
- ☐ *Arctostaphylos uva-ursi*, bearberry
- ☐ *Aristolochia californica*, Dutchman's pipe
- ☐ *Berberis* species, barberries
- ☐ *Carex tumulicola*, foothill sedge
- ☐ *Carpenteria californica*, bush anemone
- ☐ *Ceanothus* 'Centennial', Centennial ceanothus
- ☐ *Chlorogalum pomeridianum*, soap plant
- ☐ *Erythronium californicum*, fawn lily
- ☐ *Festuca californica*, California fescue
- ☐ *Fragaria vesca*, woodland strawberry
- ☐ *Garrya elliptica*, coast silk-tassel
- ☐ *Heteromeles arbutifolia*, toyon
- ☐ *Heuchera maxima*, island alum root
- ☐ *Iris* species, irises
- ☐ *Juncus patens*, California gray rush
- ☐ *Melica torreyana*, Torrey's melic
- ☐ *Nasella* species, needlegrasses
- ☐ *Polystichum munitum*, western sword fern
- ☐ *Rhamnus* species, coffeeberry, redberry
- ☐ *Ribes* species, currants
- ☐ *Rosa californica*, California wild rose
- ☐ *Salvia spathacea*, hummingbird sage
- ☐ *Satureja douglasii*, yerba buena
- ☐ *Styrax officinalis redivivus*, snowdrop bush
- ☐ *Symphoricarpos* species, snowberries

# GLOSSARY

**achene** A dry, one-seeded fruit that does not split.

**annual** A plant that completes its life cycle in one season or year.

**awn** A terminal bristle attached to a plant part.

**axil, axillary** The angle between the stem and the leaf or flower.

**basal** Relating to or situated at the base.

**berry** A fleshy fruit with one to many seeds.

**biennial** A plant that lives two years.

**blade** An expanded part of a leaf or petal.

**bloom** A flower or a whitish, fine powder covering fruits or plant parts.

**bract** A reduced leaf at the base of a flower.

**branch** A secondary woody stem growing from the trunk or main stem of a plant.

**bud** An undeveloped shoot, leaf, or flower.

**bulb** An underground storage structure consisting of a bud enclosed by thickened scales, like an onion.

**bunchgrass** A perennial grass in which the stems and leaves are clumped together in contrast to a grass that spreads by stolons or rhizomes.

**caespitose** In tufts or dense clumps.

**calyx** The sepals at the base of a flower.

**catkin** A dense spike of small flowers found on wind-pollinated trees or shrubs.

**caudex** Woody base of otherwise herbaceous perennial.

**chaparral** A vegetation type composed of dense, drought-tolerant, evergreen shrubs, adapted to a Mediterranean climate.

**cismontane** Region of California west of the Sierran crest.

**compost** Decomposed organic matter that is a fertilizer and a soil conditioner.

**compound** A leaf with two or more leaflets on a single stalk.

**conifer** A tree or shrub, usually evergreen with needlelike leaves, bearing cones rather than flowers, such as pines.

**coppice** A pruning practice that involves periodic cutting or pruning plants to the ground to encourage new growth.

**cordate** Heart-shaped, with notch at base and ovate in general outline, as the leaf of redbud.

**corm** Solid, bulblike, underground stem.

**corolla** Inner perianth of flower, composed of colored petals that may be united.

**crown** The base of a plant where roots and stem meet, and also the leaves and branches of a tree.

**culm** A hollow stem, typical of grasses.

**cultivar** A cultivated variety of a plant having desirable traits and given a non-Latin name. Cultivar names are capitalized and enclosed in single quotation marks, such as *Arctostaphylos* 'Emerald Carpet'.

**cyme** A flat-topped flower cluster.

**deadheading** Removing old flowers during the growing season to encourage the development of new flowers, improve appearance, and prevent seed formation.

**deciduous** A plant that loses all of its leaves at one time, typically in fall.

**decumbent** A plant growing near the ground with tips ascending.

**dioecious** Having male and female flowers on separate plants.

**disc flower** The small center flowers of a composite or daisy.

**dissected** A leaf divided into numerous fine segments.

**divided** Separated to the base.

**dormant, dormancy** A period of rest or inactivity that enables a plant or seed to survive conditions of drought, cold, or other stress. Plant parts above ground may wither and die back.

**drainage** The movement of water through the soil.

**drift** A group of plants planted in an informal mass.

**drupe** A fleshy, one-seeded fruit containing a stone with a kernel, such as cherry.

**ecology** The study of the relationships between plants, animals, and their environment.

**ecosystem** A community of plants, animals, and their environment, functioning as a unit.

**endemic** Restricted to a particular geographic region.

**entire** Leaves that have a smooth, undivided margin.

**ephemeral** A plant that flowers for a very short time.

**espalier** A shrub or tree that has been trained to grow flat against a wall.

**evergreen** A plant that retains some leaves all year and sheds older leaves throughout the year.

**exserted** Protruded, as in stamens or bracts.

**family** A group of plants above the category of genus, defined by characteristics of flowers and fruits. Family names usually end in –aceae, such as Asteraceae (sunflower family).

**frond** Leaf of a fern.

**fruit** Seed-bearing structure. Some fruits are pods that split open and others are fleshy.

**genus** The next category under plant family, representing a group of plant species with similar characteristics.

**glaucous** A whitish or gray-green color.

**habit** The general appearance or form of a plant (tree, shrub, vine).

**habitat** The environment in which a plant lives, including its plant community, soil, slope, and other factors.

**hardy** Plants that tolerate freezing temperatures; degree of hardiness is the minimum temperature at which a species will survive.

**head** Dense, flower cluster on a single stem, typical of flowers in the sunflower family.

**herb** A plant with no woody stem or bark.

**herbaceous** Pertaining to an herb.

**humus** Decayed organic matter.

**hybrid** A cross between two species.

**indehiscent** Not splitting open, like an achene or samara.

**indigenous** Native to a country or region.

**inferior** Lower or beneath.

**inflorescence** Arrangement of flowers, such as heads, umbels, racemes, and panicles.

**introduced** A plant brought in, accidentally or intentionally, from another part of the world.

**invasive** A plant that spreads aggressively, often by stolons or rhizomes, with the potential to take over adjacent plantings.

**lateral** Pertaining to the side of something.

**leaflet** A segment of a compound leaf.

**leaf margin** The edge of a leaf.

**lobe** A segment of a cleft leaf or petal, usually rounded.

**montane** Pertaining to the mountains.

**naturalized** A plant that grows without assistance.

**node** Joint of a stem where leaves are attached.

**nut** Hard-shelled, one-seeded fruit.

**offset** Lateral, basal shoots from which new plants can develop.

**opposite** When two leaves are paired on the stem or node.

**ovate** Oval and broader at the base.

**palmate** Divided or veined like the fingers on a hand.

**panicle** A compound raceme or branched inflorescence in which the flowers open from the bottom or center toward the top.

**pedicel** Stalk of a single flower in a cluster of flowers.

**pendant** Hanging; nodding.

**perennial** A plant that lives three or more years. The term also refers to herbaceous perennials or plants that do not become woody.

**petal** One of a series of flower parts, usually colored.

**petiole** A leaf stalk.

**pinnate** Leaflets or veins arranged like a feather.

**pistil** The female part of a flower, consisting of three parts: a swollen base (ovary) in which the seeds are produced, a slender tube (style), and the tip (stigma).

**pod** A dry, splitting fruit, like a legume.

**pollen** The fine powder made by the stamens, usually yellow, containing the male germ cells.

**pollination** The transfer of pollen from stamens to pistils. The pollen grains reach the seeds inside the ovary where fertilization takes place.

**prostrate** Growing flat on the ground.

**pubescent** Covered with short, soft hairs; downy.

**raceme** A long inflorescence with flowers arranged in pedicels along a central stalk and generally opening from the bottom upward.

**ray** The outer flowers of a composite or daisy. Each ray consists of five petals fused together into a single structure.

**recurved, reflexed** Bent downward or backward.

**rhizome** An underground stem, producing shoots on the upper side and roots on the lower side.

**root** The underground portion of a plant that anchors it and absorbs water and nutrients from the soil.

**runner** A shoot or stolon that grows along the ground, or just below the ground, forming roots and a new plant at its end.

**samara** An indehiscent winged fruit, like that of a maple.

**sclerophyllous** Hard-leaved, such as the hard, thick, generally evergreen leaves of chaparral shrubs.

**scrub** Shrubby vegetation.

**seed** The ripened ovule, usually covered with a protective coating and contained in a fruit.

**sepal** Leaflike segment of the calyx, arranged in a ring outside the petals.

**serrate** Saw-toothed, usually refers to leaves.

**sessile** Attached directly to the main stem; not stalked as a leaf with a petiole.

**shrub** A woody plant of smaller proportions than a tree with multiple branches from the base rather than a single trunk.

**species** The basic unit of plant classification, indicating the specific kind of plant.

**spike** An elongated flower cluster with individual flowers attached directly to a single stalk.

**spur** A slender, tubular elongation of the petals or sepals that contains the nectar. Columbine is an example of a flower with spurs.

**stalk** Main or supporting axis of a stem of any organ, such as a leaf or flower.

**stamen** The male parts of the flower, consisting of a stalk (filament) that supports the anther where the pollen is produced.

**stolon** A modified stem that runs along the ground, forming roots and new plants at intervals. Strawberry is an example of a plant with stolons or runners.

**subshrub** A perennial plant with woody stems at the base.

**subspecies** A naturally occurring variant of a species.

**succulent** A plant with thick fleshy leaves or stems that can store water.

**taproot** A primary root with little or no side growth, typical of oak seedlings.

**tender** Plants that do not tolerate freezing temperatures.

**tendril** A slender, coiling or twining extension of branches or leaves by which a vine grasps its support.

**terminal** At the end or top of a stem or shoot.

**tomentose** Covered with short, dense, woolly hairs.

**tree** A woody plant with one or several trunks.

**tuber** A thickened underground stem for storage of food and water, with buds where new shoots and roots develop.

**umbel** A flower cluster in which the individual flower stalks radiate from a common point, like the rays of an umbrella.

**variety** A subunit of the species or variation, such as flower color or size.

**vernal pool** A depression that holds water in winter and spring and gradually dries out by summer. Plants are often associated with vernal pools in California's grasslands.

**viability** The capacity of a seed to germinate.

**vine** A plant with slender climbing or trailing stems.

**whorl** A group of leaves or other structures that radiate from a node.

**wood** The tough inner core of a tree, shrub, or perennial vine. A woody plant has hard rather than fleshy stems.

**xeric, xerophytic** Characterized by or adapted to a limited amount of moisture.

# RESOURCES

## Books

Anderson, Kat M. *Tending the Wild: Native American Knowledge and the Management of California's Natural Resources.* Berkeley and Los Angeles: University of California Press, 2005.

Bakker, Elna. *An Island Called California.* Berkeley and Los Angeles: University of California Press, 1971.

Baldwin, Bruce, and Brent D. Mishler, eds. *Jepson Manual: Higher Plants for California, Second Edition.* Berkeley and Los Angeles: University of California Press, 2012.

Balls, Edward K. *Early Uses of California Native Plants.* Berkeley and Los Angeles: University of California Press, 1962.

Barbour, Michael, Todd Keeler, and Allan A. Schoenherr. *Terrestrial Vegetation of California, Third Edition.* Berkeley: University of California Press, 2007.

Barbour, Michael G., Bruce Pavlik, Frank Drysdale, and Susan Lindstrom. *California's Changing Landscapes: Diversity and Conservation of California Vegetation.* Sacramento: California Native Plant Society, 1993.

Barbour, Michael, Sandy Lydon, Mark Borchert, Marjorie Popper, Valerie Whitworth, and John Evarts. *Coast Redwood: A Natural and Cultural History.* Los Olivos, CA: Cachuma Press, 2001.

Bornstein, Carol, David Fross, and Bart O'Brien. *Reimagining the California Lawn: Water-Conserving Plants, Practices, and Designs.* Los Olivos, CA: Cachuma Press, 2011.

Bornstein, Carol and David Fross and Bart O'Brien. *California Native Plants for the Garden.* Los Olivos, CA: Cachuma Press, 2005.

Brenzel, Kathleen Norris, ed. *Sunset Western Garden Book.* Menlo Park, CA: Sunset Publishing Corporation.

California Department of Fish and Game. *Atlas of the Biodiversity of California.* Sacramento: California Department of Fish and Game, 2003.

Carle, David. *Introduction to Fire in California.* Berkeley and Los Angeles: University of California Press, 2008.

Carle, David. *Introduction to Water in California.* Berkeley and Los Angeles: University of California Press, 2004.

Clarke, Charlotte Bringle. *Edible and Useful Plants of California.* Berkeley and Los Angeles: University of California Press, 1977.

Connelly, Kevin. *Gardener's Guide to California Wildflowers.* Sun Valley, CA: Theodore Payne Foundation, 1991.

Crampton, Beecher. *Grasses in California.* Berkeley and Los Angeles: University of California Press, 1974.

Dallman, Peter. *Plant Life in the World's Mediterranean Climates: California, Chile, South Africa, Australia, and the Mediterranean Basin.* Berkeley and Los Angeles: California Native Plant Society Press and University of California Press, 1998.

Dreistadt, Steve H., Jack Kelly Clark, and Mary Louis Flint. *Pests of Landscape Trees and Shrubs—An Integrated Pest Management Guide.* Berkeley and Los Angeles: University of California Press, 2004.

Emery, Dara. *Seed Propagation of Native California Plants.* Santa Barbara, CA: Santa Barbara Botanic Garden, 1988.

Evens, Jules, and Ian Tait. *Introduction to California Birdlife.* Berkeley and Los Angeles: University of California Press, 2005.

Faber, Phyllis M., ed. *California's Wild Gardens.* Sacramento: California Native Plant Society, 1997.

Francis, Mark, and Andreas Reimann. *The California Landscape Garden—Ecology, Culture, and Design.* Berkeley and Los Angeles: University of California Press, 1999.

Fross, David and Dieter Wilken. *Ceanothus.* Portland, OR: Timber Press, 2006.

Gildemeister, Heidi. *Mediterranean Gardening: A Waterwise Approach.* Berkeley and Los Angeles: University of California Press, 2003.

Gilmer, Maureen. *California Wildfire Landscaping.* Dallas, TX: Taylor Publishing Company, 1994.

Gisel, Bonnie J. and Stephen J. Joseph. *Nature's Beloved Son: Rediscovering John Muir's Botanical Legacy.* Berkeley, CA: Heyday Books, 2008.

Hagen, Bruce W., Barrie D. Coate, and Keith Oldham. *Compatible Plants for Under and Around Oaks.* Sacramento: California Oak Foundation, 1991.

Halsey, Richard W. *Fire, Chaparral, and Survival in Southern California.* San Diego, CA: Sunbelt Publications, 2005.

Harlow, Nora, ed. *Plants and Landscapes for Summer-dry Climates of the San Francisco Bay Regin.* Oakland, CA: East Bay Municipal Utility District, 2004.

Harlow, Nora, and Kristin Jakob, ed. *Wild Lilies, Irises, and Grasses: Gardening with California Monocots.* Berkeley and Los Angeles: University of California Press, 2004.

Holland, V. L., and Dvaid J. Keil. *California Vegetation.* Dubuque, IA: Kendall/Hunt Publishing Company, 1995.

Keator, Glenn. *Complete Garden Guide to the Native Perennials of California.* San Francisco: Chronicle Books, 1990.

Keator, Glenn. *Complete Garden Guide to the Native Shrubs of California.* San Francisco: Chronicle Books, 1994.

Keator, Glenn, Linda Yamane, and Ann Lewis. *In Full View: Three Ways of Seeing California Native Plants.* Berkeley, CA: Heyday Books, 1995.

Keator, Glenn and Susan Bazell. *The Life of an Oak: An Intimate Portrait.* Berkeley, CA: Heyday Books.

Keator, Glenn, and Alrie Middlebrook. *Designing California Native Gardens.* Berkeley and Los Angeles: University of California Press, 2007.

Keator, Glenn. *California Plant Families West of the Sierran Crest and Deserts.* Berkeley and Los Angeles: University of California Press, 2009.

Kruckeberg, Arthur R. *Introduction to California Soils and Plants: Serpentine, Vernal Pools, and Other Geobotanical Wonders.* Berkeley and Los Angeles: University of California Press, 2006.

Labadie, Emile L. *Native Plants for Use in the California Landscape.* Sierra City, CA: Sierra City Press, 1978.

Lanner, Ronald M. *Conifers of California.* Los Olivos, CA: Cachuma Press, 1999.

Lenz, Lee. *Native Plants for California Gardens.* Claremont, CA: Rancho Santa Ana Botanic Garden, 1956.

Lightfoot, Kent G. and Otis Parrish. *California Indians and Their Environment.* Berkeley and Los Angeles: University of California Press, 2009.

Lowry, Judith Larner. *Gardening with a Wild Heart: Restoring California's Native Landscapes at Home.* Berkeley and Los Angeles: University of California Press, 1999.

Lowry, Judith Larner. *The Landscaping Ideas of Jays: A Natural History of the Backyard Restoration Garden.* Berkeley and Los Angeles: University of California Press, 2007.

McMinn, Howard E. *An Illustrated Manual of California Shrubs.* University of California Press, 1970 (first ed. 1939).

Minnich, Richard A. *California's Fading Wildflowers.* Berkeley and Los Angeles: University of California Press, 2008.

Munz, Philip A. and David D. Keck. *A California Flora and Supplement.* Berkeley and Los Angeles: University of California Press, 1973.

Munz, Philip. *California Spring Wildflowers of the Foothills, Valleys and Coasts.* Revised ed. University of California Press, 2003.

O'Brien, Bart. *California Native Plant Gardens Care and Maintenance.* Rancho Santa Ana Botanic Garden, 2000.

Ornduff, Robert, Phyllis M. Faber and Todd Keeler-Wolf. *Introduction to California Plant Life.* Berkeley and Los Angeles: University of California Press, 2003.

Pavlik, Bruce, Pamela C. Muick, Sharon G. Johnson, and Marjorie Popper. *Oaks of California.* Los Olivos, CA: Cachuma Press, 1991.

Perry, Robert C. *Landscape Plants for Western Regions.* Claremont, CA: Land Design Publishing , 1992.

Pomoroy, Elizabeth. *Theodore Payne in His Own Words: A Voice for California Native Plants.* Pasadena, CA: Theodore Payne Foundation / Many Moons Press, 2004.

Quinn, Ronald D. and Sterling C. Keeley. *Introduction to California Chaparral.* Berkeley and Los Angeles: University of California Press, 2006.

Reichard, Sarah Hayden. *The Conscientious Gardener: Cultivating a Garden Ethic.* Berkeley and Los Angeles: University of California Press, 2011.

Rountree, Lester. *Flowering Shrubs of California.* Stanford, CA: Stanford University Press, 1939.

Rountree, Lester, Edited by Lester B. Rountree. *Hardy Californians: A Woman's Life with Native Plants.* Expanded ed. Berkeley and Los Angeles: University of California Press, 2006.

Rundell, Philip and Robert Gustafson. *Introduction to the Plant Life of Southern California: Coast to Foothills.* Berkeley and Los Angeles: University of California Press, 2005.

Sawyer, John, Todd Keeler-Wolf, and Julie Evens. *A Manual of California Vegetation.* Sacramento, CA: California Native Plant Society, Second ed. 2010.

Shapiro, Art, and Timothy D. Manolis. 2007. *Field Guide to Butterflies of the San Francisco Bay and Sacramento Valley Regions.* Berkeley and Los Angeles: University of California Press.

Shoenherr, Alla. A. *A Natural History of California.* Berkeley and Los Angeles: University of California Press, 1995.

Smith, M. Nevin. *Native Treasures: Gardening with the Plants of California.* Berkeley and Los Angeles: University of California Press, 2006.

Stewart, Bob. *Common Butterflies of California.* Point Reyes Station, CA: West Coast Lady Press, 1997.

Stuart, John and John Sawyer. *The Trees and Shrubs of California.* Berkeley and Los Angeles: University of California Press, 2001.

Van Atta, Susan. *The Southern California Native Flower Garden.* Layton, UT: Gibbs Smith, 2009.

## Journals and Web Sites

Calflora Database. California native plant photos and data. www.calflora.org

California Invasive Plant Council. *Cal-IPC News.* www.caleppc.org

California Native Plant Link Exchange. Nursery information. www.cnplx.info

California Native Grass Association. *Grasslands.* www.cnga.org

California Native Plant Society. *Fremontia.* www.cnps.org

California Oak Foundation. *California Oak Report.* www.californiaoaks.org

California Society for Ecological Restoration. *Ecesis.* www.sercal.org

CalPhotos: Plants. www.calphotos.berkeley.edu

Encycloweedia. Weed information. www.cdfa.ca.gov/phpps/ipc/encycloweedia

Growing Native Research Institute. *Growing Native.* www.growingnative.com

International Plant Propagators Society. www.ipps.org

Mediterranean Garden Society. *The Mediterranean Garden.* www.mediterraneangardensociety.org

National Wildlife Federation. Backyard Wildlife Habitat Program. *National Wildlife.* www.nwf.org

Pacific Bulb Society. *The Bulb Garden.* www.pacificbulbsociety.org

Pacific Horticultural Society. *Pacific Horticulture.* www.pacifichorticulture.org

Rancho Santa Ana Botanic Garden. Claremont, CA. *Occasional publications.* www.rsabg.org

Regional Parks Botanic Garden. Berkeley, CA. *The Four Seasons* and *Manzanita.* www.nativeplants.org

Santa Barbara Botanic Garden. Santa Barbara, CA. *Newsletter.* www.sbbg.org

Society for Pacific Coast Native Iris. *Almanac.* www.pacificcoastiris.org

Theodore Payne Foundations for Wild Flowers and Native Plants. *Poppy Print.* www.theodorepayne.org

WeedRIC: UC Weed Research and Information Center. www.wric.ucdavis.edu

## Botanic Gardens

The following gardens have displays of California native plants, and those noted with an * are devoted exclusively to native plants.

Leaning Pine Arboretum
California Polytechnic State University, Department of Environmental Horticulture
1 Grand Avenue, Building 48, San Luis Obispo, CA 93407
(805) 756-1106 www.dir.gardenweb.com/directory/calpoly

Mendocino Coast Botanical Gardens
18220 North Highway 1, Fort Bragg, CA 95437
(707) 964-4352 www.gardenbythesea.org

Quail Botanical Gardens
230 Quail Gardens Drive, Encinitas, CA 92024
(760) 436-3036 www.qbgardens.com

* Rancho Santa Ana Botanic Garden
1500 North College Avenue, Claremont, CA 91711
(909) 625-8767 www.rsabg.org

* Regional Parks Botanic Garden
Wildcat Canyon Road, c/o Tilden Park, Berkeley, CA 94708
(510) 841-8732 www.nativeplants.org or www.ebparks.org/parks/bot.htm

San Francisco Botanical Garden at Strybing Arboretum
Golden Gate Park, Ninth Avenue at Lincoln Way, San Francisco, CA 94122
(415) 661-1316 www.strybing.org

San Luis Obispo Botanical Garden
El Chorro Regional Park, Highway 1, P.O. Box 4957, San Luis Obispo, CA 93403 (805) 546-3501 www.slobg.org

* Santa Barbara Botanic Garden
1212 Mission Canyon Road, Santa Barbara, CA 93105
(805) 682-4726 www.sbbg.org

University of California Botanical Garden
200 Centennial Drive, Berkeley, CA 94720 (510) 642-3343
www.botanicalgarden.berkeley.edu

University of California Davis Arboretum
One Shields Avenue, Davis, CA 95616 (530) 752-4880
www.arboretum.ucdavis.edu

University of California Santa Cruz Arboretum
1156 High Street, Santa Cruz 95064 (831) 427-2998
www.arboretum.ucsc.edu

## Sources of Plants and Seeds

In addition to the following commercial sources, the botanic gardens listed above and several CNPS chapters have plant sales at least once a year. Check nursery Web sites or call for hours and plant availability. The California Native Plant Link Exchange, www.cnplx.info, is a good source of information for finding native plants, and the California Native Plant Society website, www.cnps .org, has a list of native plant nurseries by region.

Annie's Annuals
740 Market Avenue, Richmond, CA 94801, (510) 215-1671
www.anniesannuals.com
Many native annual and perennial plants in four-inch pots.

Bay Natives
375 Alabama Street, Suite 440, San Francisco 94110, (415) 287-6755
www.baynatives.com
Online nursery; native plants for the Bay Area.

Bay View Gardens
1201 Bay Street, Santa Cruz, CA 95060, (831) 423-3656
Mail order, irises.

California Flora Nursery
Somers & D Streets, Fulton, CA 95439, (707) 528-8813
www.calfloranursery.com
Wholesale and retail native and Mediterranean plants.

Central Coast Wilds
336 Golf Club Drive, Santa Cruz, CA 95060, (831) 459-0655
www.centralcoastwilds.com
Natives for ecological restoration.

C.H. Baccus
900 Boynton Avenue, San Jose, CA 95117, (408) 244-2923
Mail order, bulbs.

Circuit Rider Productions Inc.
1919 Old Redwood Hwy, Windsor, CA 95492, (707) 838-6641
www.crpinc.org
By appointment only; wholesale and retail native plants for revegetation.

Clyde Robin Seed Co.
P.O. Box 2366, Castro Valley, CA 94546, (510) 785-0425
www.clyderobin.com
Wholesale and mail order seeds.

Conserva Seed
P.O. Box 1069, Walnut Grove, CA 95690, (916) 776-1200
www.conservaseed.com
Wholesale grass seed and contract growing for revegetation.

Cornflower Farms
P.O. Box 896, Elk Grove, CA 95759, (916) 689-1015
www.cornflowerfarms.com
Wholesale, retail, contract growing.

Elkhorn Native Plant Nursery
1957B Hwy 1, Moss Landing, CA 95039, (831) 763-1207
www.elkhornnursery.com
Wholesale, retail, contract growing.

El Nativo Growers, Inc.
200 South Peckham Road, Azusa, CA 91702, (626) 969-8449
www.espseeds.com
Wholesale, contract growing.

Environmental Seed Producers, Inc.
P.O. Box 2709, Lompoc, CA 93438, (805) 735-8888
www.espseeds.com
Wholesale seeds.

Far West Bulb Farm
14499 Lower Colfax Road, Grass Valley, CA 95945, (530) 272-4775
www.californianativebulbs.com
Mail order bulbs.

Floral Native Nursery
2511 Floral Avenue, Chico, CA 95973, (530) 892-2511
www.floralnativenursery.com
Wholesale and retail plants.

Growing Solutions
P.O. Box 30081, Santa Barbara, CA 93130, (805) 452-7561
www.solutions.org
Wholesale, contract growing.

Hartland Nursery
13737 Grand Island Road, Walnut Grove, CA 95690, (916) 775-4021
www.hartlandnursery.com
Wholesale and retail; native plants for the Central Valley.

Hedgerow Farms
21740 County Road 88, Winters, CA 95694, (530) 662-6847
www.hedgerowfarms.com
Wholesale and retail seeds; container grasses, contract growing.

Industrial Forest Associates
4886 Cottage Grove Avenue, McKinleyville, CA 95519, (708) 839-3256
Retail, native conifers.

Iris Gallery, The
33450 Little Valley Road, Fort Bragg, CA 95437, (707) 964-7971
www.allthingsiris.com
Retail, irises.

Jim Duggan Flower Nursery
638 Seabright Lane, Solana Beach, CA 92075
www.thebulbman.com
Mail order bulbs.

J.L. Hudson, Seedsman
Star Route 2, Box 337, La Honda, CA 94020-9733
www.jhudsonseeds.net
Mail order seeds.

Lake County Natives
7480 Kelsey Creek Drive, Kelseyville, CA 95451, (707) 279-2868
Wholesale and retail plants, by appointment.

Larner Seeds
P.O. Box 407, Bolinas, CA 94924, (415) 868-9407
www.larnerseeds.com
Mail order seeds, retail plants at nursery, contract growing.

Las Pilitas Nursery
3232 Las Pilitas Road, Santa Margarita, CA 93453, (805) 438-5992
www.laspilitas.com
Wholesale, retail by appointment, contract collecting and growing.
Manzanita Nursery
880 Chalk Hill Road, Solvang, CA 93463, (805 688-9692
www.manzanitanursery.com
Perennials, shrubs, trees.
Matilija Nursery
8225 Waters Road, Moorpark, CA 93021, (805) 523-8604
www.matilijanursery.com
Wholesale and retail, native plants.
Mockingbird Nursery
1670 Jackson Street, Riverside, CA 92506, (951) 780-3571
Wholesale, retail, contract growing.
Moon Mountain Wildflowers
P.O. Box 725, Carpinteria, CA 93014, (805) 684-2565
Mail order seeds.
Mostly Natives Nursery
P.O. Box 258, 27235 Hyw 1, Tomales, CA 94972, (707) 878-2009
www.mostlynatives.com
Wholesale and retail plants; coastal natives and drought-tolerant plants.
Native Here Nursery
101 Golf Course Drive, Tilden Park, Berkeley, CA 94708, (510) 549-0211
www.ebcnps.org/NativeHereHome.htm
Volunteer-operated by CNPS; local native plants, contract collecting and growing, revegetation.
Native Revival Nursery
2600 Mar Vista Drive, Aptos, CA 95003, (831) 684-1811
www.nativerevival.com
Wholesale and retail native plants.
Native Sons
379 West El Campo Road, Arroyo Grande, CA 93420, (805) 481-5996
www.nativeson.com
Wholesale, native and Mediterranean plants.
Nopalito Native Plant Nursery
4107 East Main Street, Ventura, CA 93003, (805) 844-7449
www.nopalitonursery.com
Native and Mediterranean plants.
North Coast Native Nursery
2700 Chileno Valley Road, Petaluma, CA 94953, (707) 769-1213
www.northcoastnativenursery.com
Wholesale, retail by appointment, contract growing.
Northwest Native Seed
17595 Vierra Canyon Road, #172, Prunedale, CA 93907
Catalog issued late fall, ships November-April, many hard-to-find plants, data on where collected.

Pacific Coast Seed
533 Hawthorne Place, Livermore, CA 94550, (925) 373-4417
www.pcseed.com
Wholesale seeds for restoration and revegetation; grasses, wildflowers.

Rana Creek Habitat Restoration
35351 East Carmel Valley Road, Carmel, CA 93924, (831) 659-3820
www.ranacreek.com
Wholesale, mail order, contract growing.

Reveg Edge, The
P.O. Box 609, Redwood City, CA 94064, (650) 325-7333
www.ecoseeds.com/nature.html
Mail order, contract growing, grasses and seeds.

Rosendale Nursery and Sierra Azul Nursery & Gardens
2660 East Lake Avenue, Watsonville, CA 95076, (831) 763-0939
www.sierraazul.com
Wholesale, retail, native and Mediterranean plants.

San Marcos Growers
125 South San Marcos Road, Santa Barbara, CA 93160, (805) 683-1561
www.smgrowers.com
Wholesale.

Santa Barbara Natives
16000-A Calle Real, Gaviota, CA 93117, (805) 698-4994
Wholesale, retail, contract growing.

Seedhunt
P.O. Box 96, Freedom, CA 95019, (831) 728-5131.
www.seedhunt.com
Mail order, seeds.

Specialty Oaks
12552 Highway 29, Lower Lake, CA 95457, (707) 995-2275
www.specialtyoaks.com
Wholesale, large oak trees.

Suncrest Nurseries, Inc.
400 Casserly Road, Watsonville, CA 95076, (831) 728-2595
www.suncrestnurseries.com
Wholesale plants for coastal California.

Tarweed Native Plants
4520 Dundee Drive, Los Angeles, CA 90027, (323) 663-0113
www.tarweednativeplants.com
Wholesale and retail, by appointment only.

Telos Rare Bulbs
P.O. Box 4147, Arcata, CA 95518
www.telosrarebulbs.com
Many native bulbs.

Theodore Payne Foundation
10459 Tuxford Street, Sun Valley, CA 91352, (818) 768-1802
www.theodorepayne.org
Retail plants, mail order seeds.

Tree of Life Nursery
  33201 Ortega Highway, San Juan Capistrano, CA 92693, (949) 728-0685
  www.treeoflifenursery.com
  Wholesale and retail plants, contract collecting and growing.
Watershed Nursery, The
  601-A Canal Boulevard, Richmond, CA 94804, (510) 234-2222
  www.thewatershednursery.com
  Local native plants, revegetation.
Yerba Buena Nursery
  19500 Skyline Boulevard, Woodside, CA 94062, (650) 851-1668
  www.yerbabuenanursery.com
  Large demonstration garden, all natives except for ferns.

# ART CREDITS

## Color Photographs

**ROBERT M. CASE** 106 (left), 107 (top), 111 (top), 118, 127, 141, 174 (bottom), 176 (bottom), 212 (top), 213 (top)

**KATHERINE GREENBERG** 2–4, 6, 7, 15 (bottom), 16, 18 (left), 22, 24, 25, 27, 54 (bottom), 79, 96, 140, 167, 169 (bottom), 174 (top), 182, 227 (top)

**REGIONAL PARKS BOTANIC GARDEN, COURTESY OF** i, 15, 17, 18 (right), 19, 29, 47–49, 50 (left, right), 51, 52 (top, bottom), 53, 54 (top) 55, 56, 58–60, 61 (top left, right, bottom left), 63–66, 67 (left, right), 68–70, 71 (top, bottom) 80–85, 88 (top, bottom), 89, 90, 91 (top, bottom), 93, 95, 97, 99 (top, bottom), 100–103, 105, 106 (right), 107 (bottom), 108–110, 111 (bottom), 112, 113, 115, 117, 120 (top, bottom), 122 (left, right), 123–125, 128, 129, 133, 134 (top, bottom), 136 (top, bottom), 138, 139, 142–150, 152, 153, 155–157, 158 (top, bottom), 159 (top, bottom), 162, 163, 165, 166, 167 (top, bottom), 168, 169 (top), 171–173, 176 (top), 179, 181, 183, 184, 186 (top, bottom), 187, 189 (top, bottom), 191, 193 (top, bottom), 195 (top, bottom), 196, 199, 204, 206, 207, 209, 210, 212 (bottom), 213 (bottom), 214, 215 (top, bottom), 216, 219 (top, bottom), 220, (top, bottom), 222 (top, bottom), 223 (top, bottom), 224–226, 227 (bottom), 228–231

**SAXON HOLT/PHOTOBOTANIC** Cover; ii, iii, vi, x, 1, 9, 35, 40–41, 45, 73, 131, 197, 211, 217, 281

## Maps

**MAP 1** From Hans and Pam Peeters' *Raptors of California* (2005), University of California Press.

**MAP 2** From Ronald D. Quinn and Sterling C. Keeley's *Introduction to California Chaparral* (2006), University of California Press.

## Line Illustrations

All line illustrations drawn by Beth D. Merrick.

# INDEX

# ABOUT THE AUTHORS

**Katherine Greenberg** is a fifth-generation Californian, born in Monterey County, who currently lives in Lafayette. She received a Master of Library Science at the University of California, Berkeley, and a Certificate of Landscape Design at Merritt College, Oakland. She is past president of Pacific Horticulture Society and the Mediterranean Garden Society, and founding president of the Friends of the Regional Parks Botanic Garden. She has taught classes at the Regional Parks Botanic Garden and Merritt College, and her articles have appeared in *Pacific Horticulture* and other journals. A garden designer, Katherine received a *Garden Design* Green Award for her native garden in 2010.

**Marjorie Schmidt** (1905–1989) was born in Berkeley and attended the University of California, Berkeley. Drawing upon the practical experience she gained from creating native plant gardens in Berkeley, Los Gatos, and Hayfork, she wrote a column on growing native plants for *Fremontia,* the journal of the California Native Plant Society. She also contributed articles to many other horticultural journals, including *Pacific Horticulture.* Marjorie was elected a Fellow of the California Native Plant Society, and received the Award of Merit of the American Rock Garden Society. In 1983, she received the Annual Award of the California Horticultural Society at its fiftieth anniversary meeting.

| | |
|---|---|
| Series Design: | Barbara Haines |
| Design Enhancements: | Beth Hansen |
| Composition: | Bytheway Publishing Services |
| Text: | 9/10.5 Minion |
| Display | ITC Franklin Gothic Book and Demi: |
| Prepress: | Embassy Graphics |
| Printer and Binder: | CS Graphics |